The Aesthetical Writings of Giacinto Scelsi

The Aesthetical Writings of Giacinto Scelsi

Edited and Translated by Franco Sciannameo
and Alessandra Carlotta Pellegrini

ROWMAN & LITTLEFIELD
Lanham • Boulder • New York • London

Published by Rowman & Littlefield
An imprint of The Rowman & Littlefield Publishing Group, Inc.
4501 Forbes Boulevard, Suite 200, Lanham, Maryland 20706
www.rowman.com

86-90 Paul Street, London EC2A 4NE

Copyright © 2023 by The Rowman & Littlefield Publishing Group, Inc.

All rights reserved. No part of this book may be reproduced in any form or by any electronic or mechanical means, including information storage and retrieval systems, without written permission from the publisher, except by a reviewer who may quote passages in a review.

British Library Cataloguing in Publication Information Available

Library of Congress Cataloging-in-Publication Data
Names: Scelsi, Giacinto, 1905-1988, author. | Sciannameo, Franco, editor, translator. | Pellegrini, Alessandra Carlotta, editor, translator.
Title: The aesthetical writings of Giacinto Scelsi / edited and translated by Franco Sciannameo and Alessandra Carlotta Pellegrini.
Other titles: Prose works. Selections. English
Description: Lanham : Rowman & Littlefield, 2023. | Includes bibliographical references and index. | Summary: "Giacinto Scelsi, an innovative and often controversial force in modern music, has been the subject of a vast amount of literary criticism, philosophical discussion, and performance. For the first time, this volume brings selected writings, spanning from the early 1940s to 1987, into English with historical, social, and cultural contextualization" —Provided by publisher.
Identifiers: LCCN 2022056451 (print) | LCCN 2022056452 (ebook) | ISBN 9781538166819 (cloth) | ISBN 9798881806545 (pbk) | ISBN 9781538166826 (epub)
Subjects: LCSH: Music—Philosophy and aesthetics. | Art—Aesthetics. | Scelsi, Giacinto, 1905–1988—Criticism and interpretation.
Classification: LCC ML410.S223 A25 2023 (print) | LCC ML410.S223 (ebook) | DDC 781.1/7—dc23/eng/20221129
LC record available at https://lccn.loc.gov/2022056451
LC ebook record available at https://lccn.loc.gov/2022056452

Contents

List of Figures	vii
Preface by Eric Drott	ix
Introduction and Acknowledgments	xv

PART I

Chapter	1	Prologue	3
Chapter	2	The Meaning of Music	15
Chapter	3	The Evolution of Harmony	25
Chapter	4	The Evolution of Rhythm	33
Chapter	5	Art and Satanism	43
Chapter	6	Unity and Equality of the Arts	51
Chapter	7	Epilogue	61

PART II

Chapter	8	Introduction	69
Chapter	9	Sound and Music	75
Chapter	10	Art and Knowledge	89

Conclusion	103
Bibliography	111
Discography	113
Index	147
About the Editors	155

Figures

1.1	Concert Program. Lausanne 1942 © Archivio Le parole gelate, Ampezzo	4
1.2	Scelsi's Piano Trio. *Andante* (Thematic Sketch)delete period Graphic Rendition Created by Editors	7
1.3	Scelsi's Piano Trio. *Andante* (Opening Measures) Graphic Rendition Created by Editors	8
1.4	Scelsi's Piano Trio. *Andante* (Closing Measures) Graphic Rendition created by Editors	9
9.1a	*Son et Musique.* Typescript of working draft with initial autographed emendations by Giacinto Scelsi © Fondazione Isabella Scelsi. Roma	76
9.1b	*Son et Musique.* Typescript of working draft with final autographed emendations by Giacinto Scelsi © Fondazione Isabella Scelsi. Roma	77
9.2a.	*Son et Musique.* Typescript of working draft with initial autographed emendations by Giacinto Scelsi. © Fondazione Isabella Scelsi. Roma	78
9.2b.	*Son et Musique.* Typescript of working draft with initial autographed emendations by Giacinto Scelsi. © Fondazione Isabella Scelsi. Roma	79

11.1	Scelsi's autographed sketch of *Octologo*. Page 1 © Fondazione Isabella Scelsi. Roma	106
11.2	Scelsi's autographed sketch of *Octologo*. Page 2 © Fondazione Isabella Scelsi. Roma	107
11.3	Scelsi's *Circle and Line* autographed signature © Fondazione Isabella Scelsi. Roma	108

Preface

Reading Scelsi

A book like this, which collects in one place translations of Giacinto Scelsi's writings on music, is long overdue. True, Scelsi remains something of a marginal figure in the Anglophone world, despite the growing acclaim—and controversy—surrounding his music since its "rediscovery" in the 1970s and 1980s. Indeed, at least a part of his appeal would seem to derive from the liminal position he occupies between celebrity and obscurity: his music is well-known, but only among the cognoscenti—albeit one that spans conventional musical boundaries. Thus, while Scelsi remains most closely identified with the tradition of avant-garde concert music, being a key inspiration for later generations of composers (most notably the spectralists), his influence has spread far beyond the new music scene, narrowly construed (one sign of this influence being expressed in the title to no wave/free jazz guitarist Marc Ribot's 2003 album, *Scelsi Morning*).[1] The breadth of those with an interest in his music was made abundantly clear to me at a concert of his works that I attended at Columbia University's Miller Theater in 2004. I have been to quite a few concerts of new music at the Miller before then, but never had the venue been so packed—and not just by the "usual suspects" of young composers and other new music aficionados, but with a more diverse crowd than I ever recall seeing there, or at any other new music concert, before or since.[2]

There is another, and arguably more important manner in which Scelsi remains obscure, however, which has to do with the allusive and at times cryptic way that he talked about both himself and his music. This trait was very much in force during the period of his career that has attracted the most attention from performers, critics, musicologists, and listeners, i.e., the years when his mature style came to fruition, from the 1950s on.[3] Publication of his writings on music will go some way towards remedying this issue—though with the caveat that some of his later texts (in particular "Sound and Music" and "Art and Knowledge) remain as enigmatic as ever, with their evocation of the influence of Devic activity on artistic creation; of the musician's calling to capture and "crystallize" a moment of transhuman, cosmic *durée*; of the somewhat mysterious "third dimension" of sound that European musicians have largely neglected; and so on. But if some of Scelsi's proclamations continue to defy easy explication, this studied obscurity (some might say obscurantism) is counterbalanced by the important biographical and historical context that the editors of this volume, Franco Sciannameo and Alessandra Carlotta Pellegrini, have provided in the introductions, conclusions, and interludes that stitch together Scelsi's different utterances. These interstitial texts fill in vital details about his life in Lausanne, Switzerland, during the 1940s; of performances of his compositions during the same period; of his interactions and collaborations with composers like Richard Falk; and of the arrangements he and his mother made to have his extant catalog published by Edizioni De Santis upon his return to Rome in 1945, among many other things. By situating Scelsi's music and thought within a specific, sociohistorical milieu, these biographical sketches provide a helpful counterpoint to Scelsi's own self-representations. He comes to appear as less of the singular, eccentric figure that is depicted in most accounts of his life and work, including his own, and help to bring him—if not his music—down to earth.

As for the writings themselves, they clearly fall into two distinct periods, a fact that the organization of the present volume makes clear: those that date from Scelsi's Swiss sojourn versus those composed after his return to Rome. Despite some notable continuities across this biographical and stylistic divide, the most salient difference between the writings of these two periods has to do with the kind of historical consciousness they exhibit. In the earlier writings—especially in texts like "The Evolution of Harmony" and "The Evolution of Rhythm"—Scelsi adheres to a progressive understanding of Western music's historical development. In many respects, the stories he narrates recall mainstream accounts of post-Wagnerian music, as well as broader discourses of civilizational progress popular in Western Europe in the late nineteenth and early twentieth centuries. If there is something distinctive about Scelsi's conception of musico-historical progress, it is the way it is inflected by his abiding spiritual and mystical concerns. Thus changes in harmonic language, rhythmic organization, melodic expression, and so forth, are for Scelsi not simply questions of the increasing refinement and complexification of musical technique. And this is because different aspects of music—rhythm, structure, melody, and harmony—are nothing more than the outward sonic-material expression of what for him are the defining elements of human existence: the sensorial (or vital),[4] the intellectual, the emotional, and the psychic. Musical progress thus becomes an index of not social but of spiritual progress—a key distinction in that the perfectability he envisages would apparently be restricted to a select, elect few.

Scelsi's early adherence to the form, if not the content, of then-popular liberal narratives of progress is manifest in another way, in his tendency to restrict the capacity for musical evolution to European music alone. Dynamism and change become the exclusive province of the West, while the nonwestern rest are transformed into figures of stasis and timelessness— a reductive stereotype whose baleful implications aren't lessened by the positive value he increasingly attached to these same qualities in subsequent texts. Falling back on popular tropes redolent of both contemporary race science and colonial fantasy, he divides the world into three broad types—the European, the African, and the Asian—each of which is seen to possess a particular psychic and musical disposition. One corollary of this racial-geographic partitioning of the world is a dim view of certain forms of intercultural hybridization, as seen in his remarks on jazz and jazz-inflected concert music in "The Evolution of Rhythm." But if a vulgar, commercialized form of hybridity is viewed as suspect, Scelsi nonetheless reserves space for "higher" forms of cross-cultural influence, as evinced in his own musico-spiritual practice. Whence his appropriation of certain ideas and practices of Indian and Tibetan religion, his use of historically as well as geographically exoticized titles (e.g., Ttai, Konx-Om-Pax, Hurqualia, etc.), or, more broadly, his conception of music as a means for attaining spiritual enlightenment.

In this respect, later texts like "Sound and Music" and "Art and Knowledge" stand in sharp contrast to his earlier writings. Non-European traditions no longer function as fixed points in relation to which the forward progress of musical expression—and spiritual development—can be gauged. Rather, they are held up as exemplars of precisely the kind of transcendence that Scelsi increasingly placed at the center of artistic practice. Instead of moving *forward*, there is a turning *inward*, a torsion that renders the social and historical conditions of an artwork's facture moot. "Should an Egyptian or Khmer sculpture, a Ming or Tang object be considered according to the time and period in which it was created?" Scelsi queries at one point in "Art and Knowledge." He answers his own question in the negative, claiming that "it is the intrinsic quality of the object, of the work, which only counts, that is to say the "result," the "manifestation" of the particular faculties of the creative artist." This line of argument is in keeping with Scelsi's assertion elsewhere in the same essay, that it is the artist's vocation to "arrest motion" and "crystallize an instant of duration"—though it is worth noting that if art does indeed channel a spiritual absolute, concomitant with this is a reinscription of the timeless "instant of duration" thus captured into the flow of mundane historical time. Suffice it to say that Scelsi doesn't take into account this dialectical corollary of his theory of art. Indeed, his one-sided disavowal of history has led me to interpret it elsewhere as a sublimated expression of Scelsi's class consciousness, once the growing marginalization after 1945 of the old aristocratic elite to which he belonged transformed him into something of a man out of time.[5] But whatever the root cause of Scelsi's historical pessimism, its effects are clear enough: a retreat inward, and a longing for a fantasmatic past that—ironically—resulted in music that was in many respects more innovative than his earlier music, composed at a time when he was more favorably inclined to ideas of musical innovation and progress.

The present collection represents an indispensable contribution to Scelsi studies. Yet it is still just a contribution, part of a larger project of disentangling and illuminating the relations linking man, myth, and music. As such, one would hope that it represents less of an end in itself than a new beginning, encouraging other scholars and aficionados of Scelsi's music to continue delving further into his work and his life. Much remains to be done to clarify other elements of his biography, other influences on his music and thought, the exact nature of his compositional process, his collaborations with other composers (Vlad, Tosatti, et al.), the milieus in which he moved, the reception of his music, the way it was mediated by the broader historical and social context in which it was composed—the list goes on.[6] If, for Scelsi, the task of the artist is to provide access to a transhistorical *durée*, it is the task of music historians and critics to reinsert him back into the ebb and flow of historical time, not in order to undercut the sublime qualities of his work, but in order to throw these into sharper relief. This is a task that the present volume does much to advance.

Eric Drott
Associate Professor of Music Theory
University of Texas at Austin

Notes

1. https://www.marcribot.com/scelsi-morning

2. Though it should be acknowledged that the Miller Theater only seats 700, give or take.

3. See for instance his autobiographical work, *Il sogno 101* (a cura) di Luciano Martinis e Alessandra Carlotta Pellegrini. Macerata, Quodlibet, 2010.

4. In "The Meaning of Music" and "Unity and Equality" Scelsi's term alternately refers to the sensory, physiological, or vital; by the time of "Art and Knowledge," however, he appears to have settled on vital for this element.

5. Eric Drott, "Class, Ideology, and *il caso Scelsi*," *The Musical Quarterly* 89 no. 1 (2006): 80-120.

6. It should be noted that articles published in *i suoni, le onde* . . . have done much to fill in these blanks already. See http://www.scelsi.it/it/i-suoni-le-onde/i-suoni-le-onde/.

Introduction and Acknowledgments

Giacinto Scelsi (La Spezia, 1905–Rome, 1988), Italian poet, musician, thinker, and art connoisseur, achieved a formidable status in the world of music late in life notwithstanding the unwelcoming stance assumed by some critics who felt incensed by his allegedly "unscrupulous" and even arrogant approach to compositional practices and promotion of his works. At this junction, though, Giacinto Scelsi needs no biographical introduction—especially in the wake of Eric Drott's authoritative "Preface"—to this collection of thoughts on aesthetic matters published in English for the first time as a prequel to *Music as Dream: Essays on Giacinto Scelsi* published by Rowman & Littlefield in 2013.

Originally written and/or tape recorded in French for later typing, the present essays were published in a scattered fashion under Scelsi's supervision and posthumously. *Sens de la musique* (The Meaning of Music), for instance, was written in 1942 as a text for a lecture that Scelsi delivered in Lausanne, Switzerland, prior to a performance of his music. It appeared in essay format in the January 1, 1944, issue of *Suisse Contemporaine*, a literary journal published in Lausanne. This version of the text was published in *Musik-Konzepte 31—Giacinto Scelsi*, edited by Heinz-Klaus Metzger and Rainer Riehn (München: Edition Text & Kritik, 1983). It was subsequently annotated and translated into Italian by Adriano Cremonese in 1985 on behalf of Nuova Consonanza-Le parole gelate. Finally, in 2006, *Sens de la musique* was republished in the original French in *Les anges sont ailleurs . . . Textes et inédits recuillis et Commentés par Sharon Kanach* (Arles: Actes Sud), and in German in 2013 as part of *Die Magie des Klangs*, a two-volume comprehensive edition of Scelsi's literary output that included the original French and the German translation printed side by side under the editorship of Friedrich Jaecker for MusikTexte Zeitschrift für neue Musik in Cologne. Like an afterthought, *Sens de la musique* and some of the essays that followed it reappeared in the second edition, enlarged and updated, of *Musik-Konzepte 31—Giacinto Scelsi*, edited by Heinz-Klaus Metzger and Rainer Riehn (München: Edition Text & Kritik, 2015). Thus, *Sens de la musique*, the youthful "essay before a performance" which contained the kernels of the author's aesthetic thinking, benefited from two German translations.

The divulgation of Scelsi's other essays followed a non-systematic, accidental line of planning. Adriano Cremonese was responsible for bringing to print the Italian versions of *Évolution de l'harmonie* (The Evolution of Harmony) and *Évolution du rythme* (The Evolution of Rhythm) for Fondazione Isabella Scelsi in 1992. Over a decade later, French publisher *Actes Sud*, issued in collaboration with Fondazione Isabella Scelsi three volumes dedicated to Scelsi's complete literary works. (1) *Les anges sont ailleurs . . . Textes et inédits recuillis et Commentés par Sharon Kanach*, 2006; (2) *L'homme du son: Poésies recuillis et commentées par Luciano Martinis avec la collaboration de Sharon Kanach*, 2006; (3) *Il Sogno 101: Mémoires présentés et commentés par Luciano Martinis et Alessandra Carlotta Pellegrini, sous la coordination de Sharon Kanach*, 2009. This latter volume, a French translation of the original Italian text, was included in the Kanach-Actes Sud collection for the sake of continuity with little adherence to philological criteria because the state of the Scelsi archive at the time did not allow the necessary comparative research with the original sources. On the contrary, the publication of *Il sogno 101* (with a small letter *s*), Scelsi's original autobiographical text, edited by Luciano Martinis and Alessandra Carlotta Pellegrini, saw the light in 2010 through the publisher Quodlibet in Macerata with the support of Fondazione Isabella Scelsi. This edition presented the original Italian text in its completeness supported by a rigorous critical apparatus as wished by Scelsi for posthumous publication. The Martinis-Pellegrini volume comprises two accounts of Scelsi's autobiography written in narrative and poetic form, respectively. No English translations of *Il sogno 101* are currently available. An Anglophone reading of the early aesthetical writings of Giacinto Scelsi was appended, however, to the unpublished doctoral dissertation by Gregory N. Reish titled *The Transformation of Giacinto Scelsi's Musical Style and Aesthetic, 1929–1959* (Athens: University of Georgia, 2001).

For the present collection, we have grouped Scelsi's essays in two parts according to their time of writing. Part I includes "The Meaning of Music," "The Evolution of Harmony," "The Evolution of Rhythm," "Art and Satanism," and "Unity and Equality of the Arts" (Lausanne 1942–1944), bookended by a prologue and an epilogue intended to contextualize the time and the social milieu that conditioned the gestation of these thoughts. The two essays included in part II, "Sound and Music," and "Art and Knowledge," are preserved in the archives of Fondazione Isabella Scelsi as typed transcriptions of recorded "conversations" that occurred in Rome in the early 1950s between Scelsi and a group of unidentified interlocutors. Here too, we have added an introduction and a conclusion to provide a more consistent frame of reference to the unfolding events that made Rome unique in the 1950s, a time when the so-called Economic Miracle, Fellini's cinema, and the overwhelming descent upon the Eternal City of the Hollywood film industry, made Scelsi's Rome a much different place than wartime Lausanne where the destiny of many was on the "ballot" for survival. Scelsi's stylistic approach to the two groups of thoughts is, then, remarkably different, more so if one follows the stylistic evolution of his compositions from the early neo-classicist, post-expressionist phases to the exotic, deeper concepts of sonic expressions that conflated ultimately into the single sound (*una nota sola*) philosophical exploit and its ultimate crystallization.

Our concluding comments propose a reading of Scelsi's very last aesthetic thoughts which he expressed in the form of aphorisms about the "tenets of life" outlined in the *Octologo* (1987), and the process of crystallization of his own being hermetically illustrated in geometrical shapes in *Cercles* (1986).

The editorial criteria applied to this edition of Giacinto Scelsi's aesthetic thoughts include the addition of brief introductory remarks and endnotes meant to clarify some textual ambiguities often imbued in Scelsi's original idiomatic French text. In addition, we provided the text with comparative notes highlighting some commentaries advanced by the scholars who published these essays in their French, Italian, and German editions. In doing so, we have refrained from adding another layer of literary criticism, preferring, instead, to let the reader reach unbiased conclusions about the significance of Giacinto Scelsi's little-known aesthetic thoughts when compared to the much-written-about evolution of the music that ultimately assured him a place among the most influential composers of the twentieth century.

We wish to thank Michael Tan, our acquisition editor at Rowman & Littlefield, for encouraging the publication of this book and for following every step of its making with passion and deep knowledge of the subject. Also, we thank the entire production team assigned to the realization of this project. A special thank-you goes to Professor Eric Drott of the University of Texas at Austin for having graciously agreed to preface our effort to make Scelsi's aesthetic writings known to a larger readership.

In Rome, we express our gratitude to Irmela Heimbächer, president of Fondazione Isabella Scelsi, Luciano Martinis, vice president, and the members of the Governing Council Monique Ailhaud, Wolfgang Becker, Aldo Brizzi, Stefania Gianni, Ombretta Macchi, Gianni Trovalusci, and former member Franz van Rossum. Their much-appreciated trust on behalf of our initiative has made the publication of this book possible.

Finally, we offer heartfelt thanks to Simone Caputo for contributing the essential, up-to-date discography of the works by Giacinto Scelsi, and to Louise Cavanaugh Sciannameo for her professional linguistic expertise and unlimited patience in helping to shape our manuscript as it evolved into the present form.

Franco Sciannameo and Alessandra Carlotta Pellegrini
Pittsburgh—Rome
August 2022

PART I

CHAPTER ONE

Prologue

Lausanne 1942–1944

The concert program shown below, dated *Lausanne, Thursday 11 June 1942–XX*, can be viewed by some as a reminder of a time of war, when words like persecution, final solution, exile, loss, regrets, "damaged life" as a philosopher called it, were written, spoken, and heard with regularity. Others could view the playbill as a sign that life was tolerable under the most stressful of circumstances, at least on the part of a group of privileged, fortunate individuals able to attend that concert in "neutral" Switzerland as they waited for the hostilities to cease in the surrounding countries. Ultimately, they made it out safely while millions of fellow humans vanished into eternity.

Giacinto Scelsi and his English wife, Dorothy Kate Ramsden, were among the privileged guests sheltered in Lausanne's *Hôtel de la Paix*. The couple's sojourn was secured by a deposit of ten thousand Swiss francs provided by Scelsi's maternal uncle, the Marchese Giuseppe d'Ayala Valva.

During the period between the *Anschluss* (12 March 1938) and the introduction of visas on Austrian passports, Switzerland's historical neutrality was put to the test by thousands of illegal entries being reported by the Swiss Border Patrol authorities. Then, a series of highly controversial measures were put into place to uphold Switzerland's tradition as a land of refuge even while it advocated for and carried out rejections and expulsions at the borders. Official and spied information, lively debate, and the pressures brought to bear by international organizations and allied governments encouraged Swiss leaders to take a more active stance toward those demanding asylum due to persecutions in their own country, Germany, and Austria particularly. Yet Cantonal authorities remained reluctant to expand the possibilities for accepting refugees.

It was not until 13 May 1944 that Dr. Heinrich Rothmund, Chief of the Department of Federal Justice and Police, declared to members of the American Legation in Bern that he was now "convinced that the news of Jewish extermination by the Gestapo was consistent with reality."[1] In July 1944, with his convictions confirmed after a visit to the Schaffhausen border with Germany, Rothmund published new directives which replaced those of December 1942. It admitted that the Jewish people were, indeed, in mortal danger.

The concert announced in the program shown in figure 1.1 was sponsored by the Istituto Italiano di Cultura–Losanna, one of the many IIC agencies posted around the globe by the Italian government—Fascist then (as claimed by the Roman numeral XX printed in the date) and Republican now—to promote Italian culture abroad. The event featured the music of two composers, Piero Coppola, a Milan born, Lausanne resident since 1939, and

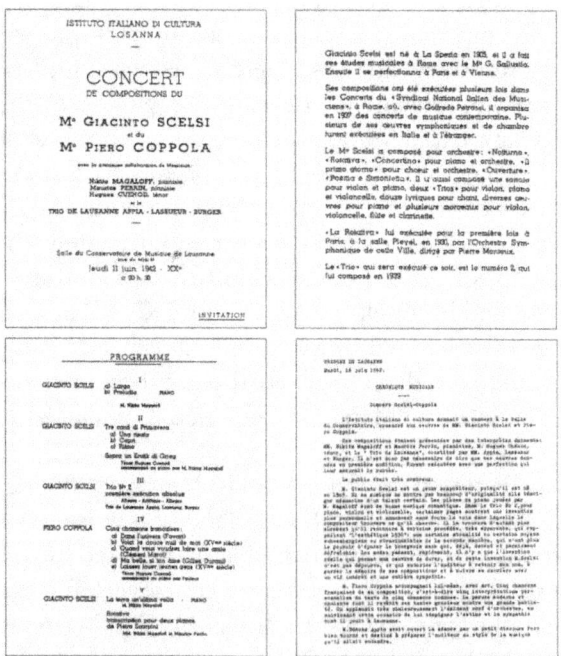

Figure 1.1. Concert Program. Lausanne 1942.
© Archivio Le parole gelate, Ampezzo

Giacinto Scelsi, a long-term paying guest of the *Hôtel de la Paix* in Lausanne where he and his socialite wife had joined a cast of extravagant characters anxiously waiting for the "all clear" heralding their safety.[2]

The concert program, tilted in favor of Scelsi's music, included compositions representing a summation of Scelsi's achievements to date under the tutelage of three professional composers: Giacinto Sallustio (1879–1938), Walther Klein (1882–1961), and Richard Falk (1878–1949). For example, *Tre canti di primavera* with lyrics by Sibilla Aleramo (1932) and *Sopra un "Erotik" di Grieg* with lyrics by Gabriele D'Annunzio (1932) for voice and piano, reveal certain crepuscular or decadent stylistic traits one may associate with Sallustio's music, judging from his few extant compositions. The three piano works listed at the top of the program, *Largo*—identifiable perhaps with the second movement of the monumental *Sonata per pianoforte* (1940–1942) that Nikita Magaloff premiered in Lausanne in 1944; the *Preludio*, likely "Preludio XI" dedicated to Magaloff and part of a set of *Dodici Preludi (prima serie) per piano* (1936–1940); and *La terra un'ultima volta* (*Une dernière fois la terre*), dedicated to Dorothy, the first of *Quattro poemi per pianoforte* (1934–1937) premiered by Ornella Puliti Santoliquido in Rome in 1937. They reflect the "expressive atonality," style that Scelsi developed while studying with Klein.[3] Then, the program concluded with some heavy keyboard "hammering" generated by a new version of *Rotativa* (1930) transcribed for two pianos by Pietro Scarpini and executed by Magaloff and Maurice Perrin.[4]

Such a display of virtuosity, though, and the "neo-archaic" *Cinq chansons françaises* by Piero Coppola, constituted an exciting series of "appetizers" to the prime focus of the evening: the world premiere of Scelsi's *Trio No. 2 per Violino, Violoncello e Pianoforte* (1939) performed by the Trio de Lausanne composed by violinist Edmond Appia, cellist Paul Burger, and pianist Charles Lassueur.

Scelsi's "expressive atonality," a blend of advanced chromaticism influenced by Scriabin's mysticism and Alban Berg's serial lyricism was well displayed in the solo piano works in the program not only as the result of Walther Klein's teaching, but also Magaloff's influence on Scelsi which was not limited to piano virtuosity but extended to the actual writing for the instrument as well, besides their profound friendship.

The Piano Trio, on the other hand, showed gestural characteristics and textural transparencies novel to Scelsi's music, the effect, one may conclude, of his little-known collaboration with the German-born composer Richard Falk with whom Scelsi worked between the mid 1930s and the yearly 1940s. A closer look at Richard Falk and his relationship with Scelsi is warranted.[5]

An impassioned scholar of Baroque and early classical Italian opera, Falk trained at the Leipzig Conservatory under Hugo Reimann, Salomon Jadassohn, and Arthur Nikisch. He moved to Rome in the early 1930s to assist Duke Filippo Caffarelli in bringing to fruition an ambitious project: the twenty-six-volume edition of Giovan Battista Pergolesi's *Opera Omnia*, and the creation of the *Società Amici della Musica da Camera* as the institution that sponsored the project.

Caffarelli, a wealthy, staunch music connoisseur with connections in high places, and Falk, a gifted composer with the propensity to circumvent the rigor of musicological quest for authenticity, preferred to "compose" in the style of Pergolesi when gaps needed to be filled. In sum, Falk was the perfect match to Caffarelli who wanted to see his Pergolesi dream come true by any means. So, the twenty-six-volume set of Pergolesi's *Opera Omnia* was published in installments between 1936 and 1941. Caffarelli's volumes are still circulating nowadays despite the enormous amount of criticism they elicited upon their release and later when they were further scrutinized.[6]

Richard Falk's willingness to extend his musical services to others caught the attention of Giacinto Scelsi as soon as the German composer began to work for Caffarelli. In fact, Falk's name appeared several times in the correspondence exchanged between Scelsi and his mother, donna Giovanna Scelsi d'Ayala Valva.[7] Here are some excerpts: on 14 October 1936 Scelsi informed his mother that while Sallustio was in the habit of imparting his "lessons" every afternoon, Falk preferred to visit him twice a week in the morning. Four days later, Scelsi wrote that the newspapers in Rome had announced the 1936–1937 concert season at the *Augusteo* (Rome's Teatro Adriano) which included the performance of Sallustio's symphonic tryptic *Trasfigurazioni*. Then, he added that he and Sallustio were working on "the little piano piece taken from the *Danseuse*" while he was occupied with Falk on fixing the Trio for Piano, Violin, and Cello.[8] Later in 1938, after Falk, who was a Jew, emigrated to New York because of the implementation of the Racial Law by the Italian government, Scelsi asked his mother to bring him "Falk's Trio," referring, one would think, to the Trio performed in 1937 or to the sketches pertaining to the new work, which bore the date "1939" at the time of its premiere in Lausanne in 1942 as Trio No. 2. Now, if we consider that the Trio No. 2 was dated or retro dated 1939 according to the information printed in the 1942 Lausanne concert program, Falk and Scelsi must have worked on this composition for over three years. The protracted task could have consisted of the reworking of the *Preludio e Fuga* (Trio No. 1) into the first and third movements of Trio No. 2 with the addition of a second movement. Some letters from New York written by Falk in 1940 validated such a timetable. Falk wrote: "I am very busy with the *Andante*, unfortunately though I cannot forge ahead with its elaboration as I would wish . . . there are too many problems, but half is completed, and I think that its development is beautiful and interesting." The assumption here is that the *Andante* in question was the second movement of the new Trio (No. 2). Later Falk wrote: "In the Trio (*Andante*) I have noted down the following: this movement must mature well before I send you the copy in the coming days when I think I can complete the work." Ultimately, Falk added: "Be assured that all is proceeding well with the *Andante*—also, the sketch which I wrote in a half hour—is long enough—but patience is needed for its elaboration." This sketch or part of it was probably the one penciled on the back of the envelope containing the letter sent to Scelsi and received by the post office in Rome on 11 December 1940 according to the postal seal affixed on the envelope (see facsimile of the original envelope in Sciannameo-Pellegrini 2013, 117).

Although figure 1.2 demonstrates that the material of the four-measure sketch is identical to its ultimate realizations seen in figures 1.3 and 1.4, it functioned as the opening and closing statement bookending the *Andante* proper which begins at measure five in the form of a fifteen-measure passacaglia theme (see its beginning in figure 1.3) followed by seven elaborate episodes before returning to the passacaglia theme and the closing statement.[9] The structure of this movement confirms Falk's preoccupation with its development, the challenges involved, and his professional commitment to provide Scelsi with a composition he would be proud of.

The Trio's first and third movements, on the other hand, echo the gestural "Grand Manner" so dear to the Romantics which appears every so often in Scelsi's piano music of the late 1930s and early 1940s. Thus, the stylistic inconsistencies between the first and third movements versus the *Andante*.

Figure 1.2. Scelsi's Piano Trio. *Andante* (Thematic Sketch).
Graphic Rendition Created by Editors

Figure 1.3. Scelsi's Piano Trio. *Andante* **(Opening Measures).**
Graphic Rendition Created by Editors

The music critic of the *Tribune de Lausanne* reported on Tuesday, 16 June 1942, that Edmond Appia, the renown Lausanne violinist, conductor, and distant cousin of legendary Wagnerian scenographer Adolphe Appia, delivered some remarks on the composition and aesthetic of the music on the program before a packed Salle du Conservatoire de Musique. The critic did not specify, however, what Appia said about Scelsi's Trio whose world premiere he was about to perform, but he, the critic, cared to report that,

Figure 1.4. Scelsi's Piano Trio. *Andante* (Closing Measures).
Graphic Rendition Created by Editors

certain pages of the Trio show a more personal invention than the other works by Scelsi heard in the program. Undoubtedly, they forecast the manner through which the composer will find what he is searching for; a search that will be more successful if he renounces certain processes, very apparent, which recall "the aesthetics of the 1930," i.e., a certain atonality common to certain works of Schoenberg or the Stravinsky of the second period, which no longer have the power to impress the bourgeois class but which appear to be already dated and faded. Fashions pass quickly, it is only real invention that allows works to last, and M. Scelsi possesses the qualities that may allow the listener to remember his name, his compositions and to follow his career with keen interest and full sympathy.[10]

The positive reaction placed Scelsi in good standing in the Lausanne musical community as well as in the more restricted circle of aestheticians following the lecture titled *Sens de la Musique* (The Meaning of Music) he delivered at the Conservatoire prior to the 11 June evening performance.[11]

In sum, the *Trio No. 2 per violino, violoncello e pianoforte* and *Sens de la Musique* constituted a strong assessment of Scelsi's intellectual and creative potential portentous of things to come. The original typescript text of the lecture reads in English as follows:

It is very fashionable nowadays to explain to the public the intentions, the aesthetic, or the technique involved in a new work. No doubt that such is the reason why at the concert this evening, Edmond Appia will say a few words about my Trio that you will hear shortly afterward. No one could be more qualified than he for such a task. Rarely, have I come across someone gifted as Appia with such precise and subtle understanding of the problems and the essence of modern music.

Personally, I consider any explanation of a musical work to be a nearly impossible *tour de force*, because—deep down—discussions about form, structure, diatonic or chromatic character, vertical or horizontal writing, harmonic aggregations and superimpositions, polyphony, atonality, or polytonality, mean very little.

What kinds of relationships among these elements is the public supposed to detect; technical terms and emotions, or the sensations and images envisioned by the composer? So, if we add to technicalities words praising the author's noble and profound thoughts, his astonishing freshness, poignant nuances, spontaneity, or about his slightly morbid cerebralism, how can the listener apprehend such expressions, and their relationships among the values that we attempt to explain? It should be, above all, a matter of giving the public the "key" to these connections.

Before explaining any composition, it is necessary to recognize only those relationships deemed fundamental for the understanding of all ancient and modern music. Obviously, people may ignore them and continue to listen to music whether they love it or not. They can understand and interpret it at their pleasure independent from the essence and real significance of the work. So, in this case, all explanations are useless. However, it is possible to achieve a more precise and objective understanding of music by establishing relationships between the elements that form it: rhythm, melody, harmony, and structure, which also constitute the elements' particular means of expression, and are the foundation of humankind: rhythm, emotionality, intelligence, and psyche.

Since it will not be possible to discuss or analyze these four fundamental elements during this lecture, I would just mention, instead, that it is through rhythm that human beings partake in the life of the universe, which is primal creative force, vital momentum, and continuous flux of time. It is through emotionality that passions come to life and travel cosmically through the human body. Pleasures and sufferings, points of fusion, contrasts of spirit and flesh, and of dreams and reality are all inscribed in human emotionality. It is through cognition that people choose, organize, and turn their emotional and spiritual experiences into communicable forms. It is through the psyche that they join the spheres of spiritualism, magic, metaphysic, universal consciousness, dreams, blood and ancestral memory. It is also through the psyche that people let subjective time rejoin the absolute time and beyond as eternity unfolds onto another state of existence.

The ever-changing balance ratio between these four elements determines some human expressions, and, in the world of art, some achievements or research in a given direction. The current knowledge of the psychological sciences, research on the origin of images, on automatism and so on, make it possible to distinguish, at least, some categories of images and to partially recognize their origin if not gain a closer knowledge of the mystery of the primal creative force and dynamism, which is just as insoluble as the mystery of life itself, perhaps.

Each fundamental element of mankind creates images; their different categories are expressions and therefore particular to each element. I cannot attempt here to make a careful examination of these categories, but I say to you that the categories emanating from the emotional and psychic elements—reflected in music through melody and harmony—and the emotional reactions and images provoked by them, are more immediately direct because they possess a more evident casual character. Categories belonging to a psychological order, on the other hand, have always more obscure, less identifiable origins as their manifestations are most unexpected and disconcerting. Hence, aside from the dreamlike images of a purely psychic order, the feelings and the emotional reactions rooted in the subconscious do not react instantly but emerge only sporadically by effect of uncontrollable resonance. Thus, they can be considered psychic images emerging also unexpectedly and disconcertingly in time and space but under diverse forms. In other words, if the emotional images and reactions are direct, the psychic images are not. In a certain sense, their difference is comparable to two categories of painters or two styles of painting; one reproduces objects or nature as such or as they strike the artist's sensibility, the other transforms the work into a starting point for the artist to achieve a totally personal and transfigured realization. It is this last aspect that appears most often in music as well as in poetry, painting, or sculpture, because of the quasi-total dominance assumed by the psychic and rhythmic elements in contemporary art.

Clearly, there is no lack of intellectual elements in today's art. It would seem impossible, but it is, so to speak, at the service of and suborned to the other elements. It works especially while researching technical means of materialization, realization, and expression of states created by rhythmic and psychic impulses. This very challenging research work requires a sustained effort which reveals its obvious speculative or technical nature. Hence the current false interpretation of intellectualism in modern art. The emotional element is also part of this category. Melody, although not absent in contemporary works, is almost always created, and conditioned by harmony to the point that one could say that if melody was at one time being harmonized, it is now harmony that is being most often melodized. I cannot trace here the history of this evolution that began at the end of the last century when the orientation of melody and harmony—rational and emotional for a hundred years—went through a gradual process of transformation.

The balance of the four elements; rhythm, emotionality, intelligence, and psyche, shifted in favor of the psychic and the rhythmic elements in order to provoke an anti-intellectual and anti-emotional reaction. It is not possible to analyze and examine here the reasons of this reaction whose causes took many forms: from neo-spiritualism to theosophy, from metapsychic to the popularization and propagation of Asian philosophies and doctrines, from the revalorization of intuition to the exploration of the subconscious and dreaming, from the discovery of African art, and earlier to the vogue for Afro-American music, from the rebirth of a cult of the human body to the exaltation of collective values, from the discovery of relativity to non-Euclidian geometry.

In all fields of inquiry, a new and different conception of matter, life, and becoming took shape. It abolished the old oppositions and dualisms and led to the idea of identity of matter and spirit in the form of energy and of duration that propelled the conception of a universal, transcendent psychic unity. In art as in science, in philosophy or in politics this orientation shifted toward the psychic and the rhythmic. Trends and research shared their efforts in discovering and expressing a new dimension. Conscious or unconscious re-searchability of time, space, and duration appeared in all forms. In music, it was through rhythm and harmony that this orientation manifested and expressed itself, and it was through the concurrent extraordinary and logic evolution of these two elements that a research characteristic of the contemporary spirit began to take shape.

Modern art is, therefore, the legitimate expression of this current orientation, determined by the balance ratio between the fundamental elements. Technically, it is the development and logical continuation of all antecedent art movements that mirrored mankind as the sum of legacies and the continuation of past generations. On the other hand, this orientation is in no way superior or inferior to the previous ones, or to those to follow. Time, space, dreams, duration, rhythm are all parts of our being, which can lead to states of consciousness as real and acute as those caused by joy, sadness, or pain. In art, however, it is not the degree of the attained intensity that counts. Whether art is classical or romantic, religious, or secular, realist or abstract, objective, or subjective, it matters not. The ultimate goal of art, and that of the conscious or unconscious artist, is to stop the subtraction of subjective time and restore it to his own duration through an effort of incredible intensity. Then, a sensation, an emotion, a state of consciousness crystallized in a verbal, sound, or plastic material, will flash before the amazed eyes of the world like an instant of becoming in absolute time, eternity.

Two years later, an expanded version of *Sens de la Musique* was published in the January 1944 issue of the journal *Suisse Contemporaine*. This important text was published in German by Heinz-Klaus Metzger in 1983 (hereafter Metzger 1983), in the original French by Adriano Cremonese in 1985 (hereafter Cremonese 1985), by Sharon Kanach in 2006 (hereafter Kanach 2006) which included a comparative analysis of the 1942 and 1944 versions, and in French and German by Friedrich Jaecker in 2013 (hereafter Jaecker 2013). Furthermore, Metzger 1983 was reissued in 2015.[12]

The English translation published next will aid the reader in appreciating the genuineness of the 1942 original text and the aggregate notions added by Scelsi and/or his editors for the 1944 published version.

Notes

1. Rothmund had taken it upon himself to preserve Switzerland's "purity" from "foreign-thinking" elements. Alfred A. Hasler, author of *The Lifeboat Is Full: Switzerland and the Refugees, 1933–1945* (Funk & Wagnalls, 1969), exposed the response of the Swiss people and bureaucracy to the plight of the refugees fleeing Hitler's Germany. He wrote that Dr. Rothmund returned 2,600 men, women, and children to certain death in the land they had fled, flagrantly violating the sanctity of neutrality. In a despicably clear case of aiding and abetting the Nazi regime, Rothmund suggested to the German government that German Jews be identified by stamping a red letter "J" on their passports. See also Leo Bretholz, "A Victim of Swiss History Remembers One of Its Righteous," in *The Baltimore Sun*, 21 April 1997 [https://www.baltimoresun.com/news/bs-xpm-1997-04-21-7901010129-story.html] accessed May 20, 2022.

2. Piero Coppola (Milan, 1888–Lausanne, 1971) was a well-known conductor, composer, and pianist who had fled Paris as the pro-Nazis Vichy government was installed. Apparently, he had imparted composition lessons to the Marchese Giuseppe d'Ayala Valva, an ardent Wagnerite. During her sojourn at the *Hotel de la Paix* following her marriage to Giacinto Scelsi in Geneva on 4 June 1940, Dorothy Kate Ramsden, a British socialite, novelist, and former wife of Marchese Demetrio Imperiali dei Principi di Francavilla, penned *Randolph's Folly* (Sampson Low, Marston & Company Limited, London, 1945), a novel based on the lives and mores of the cosmopolitan society in-waiting in and around Lausanne during the war. See Agnese Toniutti, "Randolph's Folly. Un romanzo di Dorothy Kate Ramsden" in *i suoni, le onde . . .* Rivista della Fondazione Isabella Scelsi 16, 2006, 10–13.

3. See Franco Sciannameo, "Expressive Atonality," in Sciannameo-Pellegrini (eds.), *Music as Dream* (2013), 95–106.

4. See Alessandra Carlotta Pellegrini, "About and Around *Rotativa*: A Look at Young Scelsi," in Sciannameo-Pellegrini (eds.), *Music as Dream* (2013), 121–142.

5. See Norman C. Thibodeau, "Richard Falk and His Performing Adaptations of Eighteenth-Century Opera." Unpublished Master Essay (The Peabody Institute of The John Hopkins University, 1990), and Luciano Martinis, "A Forgotten Personage: Richard Falk," in Sciannameo-Pellegrini (eds.), *Music as Dream*, 113–120.

6. See Thibodeau, *op. cit.*, for details about the Caffarelli-Pergolesi project and Falk's involvement in it.

7. See Martinis, *op. cit.*

8. The piano piece in question was probably based on *La Danse* for piano, a work Scelsi dedicated to Anna Pavlova, in 1931. The reference to the "Trio" could have been addressed either to the *Preludio e Fuga* per piano, violino e violoncello (1936) premiered in Rome in 1937 by Riccardo Castagnone, piano, Enrico Pierangeli, violin, and Massimo Amfiteatroff, cello, or the new Trio discussed later.

9. All references to this composition are based on the published version of the Trio (Edizioni De Santis, Roma 1947) which is no longer indicated as No. 2. This and other compositions belonging to the Scelsi Lausanne period were published in Rome by Edizioni De Santis in the late 1940s upon Scelsi's return to the Italian capital. Some of them are currently available from EDIPAN Edizioni Musicali, Roma.

10. See Adriano Cremonese, "A proposito di due inediti di Giacinto Scelsi" in *i suoni, le onde* . . . Rivista della Fondazione Isabella Scelsi 2, 1991, 14–18.

11. See facsimile of the original typescript in Cremonese, *Ibid.*

12. *Musik-Konzepte 31–Giacinto Scelsi*, edited by Heinz-Klaus Metzger and Rainer Riehn (München: Edition Text & Kritik, 1983), Second Edition, enlarged and updated, 2015. Giacinto Scelsi, A cura di Adriano Cremonese. It includes most of the texts from *Musik-Konzepte 31* translated into Italian (Roma: Le parole gelate, 1985). *Giacinto Scelsi. Les anges sont ailleurs . . . Textes et inédits recuillis et commentés par Sharon Kanach* (Arles: Actes Sud, 2006), 87–98. Giacinto Scelsi, *Die Magie des Klangs* – Gesammelte Schriften, Band 2, herausgeben von Friedrich Jaecker (Köln: Edition MusikText, 2013), 500–519.

CHAPTER TWO

The Meaning of Music

It is fashionable nowadays to provide concertgoers and listeners of radio programs with some information about the aesthetic or the technique pertinent to a new musical work by means of a text inserted in the handbill or a few words enunciated by a radio "speaker." The audience or listener is informed, therefore, about the work's classical, romantic, or modern orientation, its provenance, school, and style. Such a practice seems satisfactory to justify the scope. However, since music is, on the one hand, a sound element and, on the other—like art in general—a projection of images or states of consciousness, disquisitions about form and construction, diatonic or chromatic character, chordal structure, aggregates or harmonic superpositions, atonality or polytonality say nothing or almost nothing. General indications about the "noble and profound thought" of the author, his "freshness," "poignant accents," "spontaneity," or "cerebralism," also add nothing to the actual understanding of the work. What rapport can the audience establish between these human expressions and the technical elements by which the composer struggles to explain his work? How does the latter embody and represent the former? Without disregarding by any means the great value of many writings about music or musicians, and many a study or research on their intimate feelings and sources of inspiration, we have always thought that, in this regard, interpretations of their works were largely unsatisfactory for the reasons explained above. Until we recognize and establish the only relationships as fundamental to the understanding of all music, ancient or modern, the relationships between the elements that constitute music and the types of images projected by the composer through the sound matter, each attempt to analyze or explain the real meaning of a work seems to us extremely difficult. In our opinion, the current level of knowledge enables us to establish these relationships and arrive at a more accurate and objective understanding of music.

Without attempting to summarize the work and research of modern psychology on creative or imaginative activity, let us say that it is possible to distinguish four fundamental elements through which the human being interacts with the universe: rhythm, emotion, intellect, and psyche. We do not know the essence of these fundamental forces, but they seem to move through the human being constantly through an uninterrupted flux of vibrations whose intensity of speed is uneven and variable. Through his sensitivity the human being registers a greater or smaller part of these vibrations which he recognizes or identifies as sensations, emotions, psychic states, and images. However, sensations, emotions, and psychic states are nothing but virtual images, remainders of those unrecognized, unidentified, or even unclassified vibrations. Indeed, these remainders can produce states of consciousness of the same nature and can move across the realm of the unknown to the known in an instant.

Therefore, the word "image" is not justified when applied to music. Even if music does not pass through the filter of the intellect, neither identifying nor defining, it still expresses a part, and maybe the greater part of images produced in the consciousness by the creative forces. Before we move on to examining various types of images, it should be said that they are nothing but the creation and particular expression of the four elements mentioned above.

So, one can find in each artistic expression the manifestation of these creative forces in various forms. If we remain in the realm of music, we may say that rhythm, emotion, intellect, and psyche find their correspondents in rhythm, melody, form or structure, and harmony.

Rhythm, which one can essentially define as an alternation of thrusts, is in musical terms an alternation of sound and silence. It is also the primal impulse without which life or art would not be possible. In an organic life reduced to its simplest physical expression, one can envision the absence of one or more of the other elements but not the absence of rhythm, the vital pulse. Similarly in music, rhythm seems to be able to exist, at a certain point, independently from the other elements (for instance, rhythm generated by a drum, a wooden instrument, or a gong, struck repeatedly without accompaniment). Rhythmic language is thus the expression of profound rhythms emerging from the dynamism of life. But rhythm is also expression and manifestation of duration. So, if, on the one hand, it is the prime condition for the existence of a human being or a work of art; on the other hand, rhythm unifies and connects by its essence the personal, relative time of the creative artist and the created images to cosmic duration, to absolute time. Obviously, an intellectual construction, an arbitrary succession of rhythmic cells has nothing to do with the true meaning of rhythm, which is, first and foremost, primordial physical propulsion.

Melody is the expression of emotion. A more ancient and in a sense a simpler element than harmony, melody is the expression of emotional reactions in human beings most directly conscious after those belonging to the rhythmic order. This is because affective emotions are more immediate, more direct; they have a more causal character than those originating from the intellectual or psychic realms. Melody is inconceivable without rhythm, like emotion cannot be conceived without life. It necessitates rhythmic élan, as much as emotion of the vital pulse. Harmony is the expression of the psychic element. Thus, it goes without saying that this is not a question of "harmony" resulting from the coincidence of two or more melodic or rhythmic lines.

Chords and harmonic combinations codified by the "science of harmony" or counterpoint belong to an intellectual construct and cannot be considered real and direct psychological expressions. Harmony is the expression of images of more obscure provenance, thus less identifiable. These images are more unexpected and disconcerting, not only those of dreamlike stance or belonging to the natural order of the psyche, which are, therefore, easily recognizable, but also for the sensations and images of the rhythmic and emotional order, which having passed through the subconscious, reappear often after a long time through the effect of resonance or by an incontrollable intertwining. Then these images emerge unexpected and disconcerting, not only in time but also in space, namely in their own form. In other words, if affective images can be considered direct, those of psychic nature are indirect.

The intellect manifests and materializes itself in structure. It recognizes and establishes relationships as an identifying faculty tending toward a conceptualized structure through successive rational operations. Like rhythm or harmony, the intellectual element can appear, at a certain point independently of the other elements because of its purely rational operations, which establishes new relationships each time between identified objects and proceeding with mental operations proper and characteristic to their nature. Such a process allows the intellectual element to realize constructions based on physical laws or imitations thereof. Great constructions could be conceived by the integral expression of the intellectual element.

If it is possible to recognize and analyze these four elements separately, it is evident and almost superfluous to say that there exists no separation or interruption between them. On the contrary, one finds a constant interdependence, interference, and intertwining.

As we have said, rhythm can exist independently of the other elements up to a point. In reality, a single sound already produces a series of harmonics that constitutes somewhat a melodic element. Moreover, the variation of intensity of a sound causes a fluctuation in its pitch which provokes interference and a different relationship with the melodic element. As soon as a rhythm is no longer struck on one single note, it forms a rudimentary but perceivable melody (striking, for example, two drums of different sizes) whereas its related harmonics form a kind of polyphony through simultaneous crossings and encountering melodic lines, whose resulting sounds and chords constitute yet more interferences between rhythm and the other elements. The rhythmic element does not necessarily always manifest itself in its integral form. It is at the core of the activity of every other element, and it may appear sometimes relatively subordinated to affectivity, intellect, or psychism. In this case, rhythm loses some of its character, significance, and real force. Still, thanks to the primal impulse of the original rhythmic cells and its quality of "duration," it forms an indispensable basis for the expressions of other elements. One might also say the same about all possible balance of relationships existing between the melodic element and the others. When, for instance, the emotional expression is closely connected to the more specifically physical domain, the melodic interval and the rhythmic dynamism come together intimately and appear to possess equal importance. When, on the contrary, the affective expression approaches the intellectual or psychic level, the melodic intervals disengage, at a certain point, from the rhythmic dynamism and generate emancipated melodic lines just like human emotions can emancipate from life. There are, therefore, infinite nuances in the nature of melody like a whole possible gamut beginning with the affective expression from the nearest of the rhythmic element to the nearest of the intellectual and psychic element, just like nuances of emotions affect the human being.

The intertwining relationships between melody and harmony are just as natural as those between melody and rhythm because every melody creates chords or harmonies, as conversely every chord contains a melody. Moreover, melody calls most often for harmony, it awakens it—so to speak—like harmonies induce and awakens melodies, relationships that correspond exactly to those existing between affective and psychic emotions. There are even more subtle relationships attributed to associations of images and correspondences whose laws are unknown and that appear to have resulted in some transpositions of language. Also, all types of relationships exist between rhythm and harmony. If rhythm is at the core of all activity because of its primal impulse, harmony is less subject to it than melody, just as the mind is less bound and dependent to physiological activity than emotions. Harmony contains rhythm, and if a chord can appear to be at first independent of the rhythmic factor, it is because we forget that it is an expression of psychic images included in the duration. But it is in the succession of harmonies in time that the entire gamut of possibilities and relationships appears once again. In effect, when psychic images are close to the physiological and earthly realm, or fuse with those images that have emerged from the rhythmic element, we see harmony and rhythm dominating or appearing alternatively in certain characteristic superpositions. If, on the contrary, the images are of a purely psychic order, the successions of chords or groupings of sonorities may appear unbound by dynamism, freer of rhythm than melody could ever be. In that case, harmony regains, in essence, the rhythmic principle of duration. Equally subtle are the relationships between harmony and melody. When psychic images approach or participate in affectivity, we notice an infiltration of the melodic element in the chords, manifesting itself in their individual throughout their progression. If, on the contrary, the psychic expression is fully independent or, to be more precise, as independent as any other element can be, harmony appears just as free from both the rhythmic dynamism and the melody, and it appears to be completely irrational in the formation of aggregates and groupings of sonorities, their progressions. The relationships between the other elements bear the same characteristic of constant interchanging we have recognized among rhythm, melody, and harmony; all the relationships of balance exist in relation to these elements.

The variable intensity of the input or intervention of the intellectual element manifests itself by the degree of importance that the structure assumes in a work of art or, inversely, by the degree of realization reached by the other elements in their manifestation, that is to say, in the greater or lesser emancipation of their language by the intellectual filter and the rational elements. When rhythm or psychism are the dominant elements (as is the case in most of today's artistic expressions), structure and all intellectual constructs appear secondary or discarded, because images are projected without having passed through the filter of reason and its procedures. These images remain confined, in extreme cases, within their own limits and dimensions, logic and illogic. In this case, the role of the intellect is limited to the activity of identifying and establishing relationships and methods; in other words, of the means that allow the manifestation and the realization of the other elements, by which the function of the intellect is realized only in part, yet natural to it and at the core of its activity. Because the intellect leans by its very nature toward construction, "system," and structure. Thus, when the intensity of the creative impulses burst the established mold for containing the matter, the expression and the manifestation of these impulses produce new forms, thus destroying the precedent. Then, the intellectual element, by virtue of its particular faculties, begins to reconstruct and to form new schemas once again. Obviously, we can continue listening to music, whether we enjoy it or not, understanding and interpreting it independently of the real significance of the composition. In this case, all explanation is superfluous (except, maybe, for what descriptive music is concerned), because such music acts automatically, by its very nature on the listener's sensitivity. But if we recognize the necessity, through the human being's objective understanding, of not limiting ourselves to intuitive impressions and of pursuing specific research on the human mechanism for the benefit of a more precise interpretation of its activities and various manifestations, then a more focused understanding of artistic creations would be equally necessary for the objective comprehension of their real essence and significance.

In conclusion, let it be said that all art is nothing but projection of images onto matter, be it verbal, sound, or plastic, of images created by the fundamental elements. Through the analysis of these elements in a work of art, we discover that the artist's creative impulses are externalized and crystallized. The variation in intensity of the fundamental elements is what causes the shift in their balance relationship. A different balance is determined every time by a particular human orientation and by various artistic expressions. In other words, each work, each aesthetic, each art is determined by the projection of images resulting from the balance of the fundamental elements.

It is advisable that we examine from this angle not only works and artistic realizations for the sake of their individual expression or particular characteristics, but also any general or collective orientation occurring in the course of the historical evolution of art.

Afterword (by the Editors)

Scelsi's essay did not go unobserved. In fact, André Tanner, a well-reputed Swiss literary critic, and Rudolf Steiner scholar, "responded" to Scelsi's aesthetical assertions by penning a rebuttal in the form of a letter which was published in the May 1944 issue of *Suisse contemporaine*.[1]

He wrote:

"Dear friend,

"Your article brings to memory our previous discussions. Would this be a good opportunity to reminisce about them? If so, the only motive would be to offer a clear definition of when exactly our voices parted to opposite directions. Is our very dissent, though, anything other than an expected, passionate—yet fleeting—understanding? If not, how can we explain the singular pleasure we take in contradicting ourselves?

"I think of you as a musician who, unlike the one described by La Bruyère,[2] does not give up his soul and spirit at the same time as his instrument without satisfying the almost unconscious function of the creative faculty. I recognize in the idea that you express alternately by means of sound or speech, the sign of a cardinal virtue of our time: consciousness in creation. But should I too desire to express an idea, you would know how wary I feel about concrete and abstract ideas as they are fatal to creation. What I truly love are concrete and vibrant ideas, i.e., creation itself. This is the reason why I entertain with reservation your desire 'to arrive at a more *objective* understanding of music.' I am fully aware that a sonata cannot be an 'object' to be taken apart like a mechanical engine. I am fully aware of the passion of others only through the most personal of my own feelings, on condition that I free myself from them and move on. Therefore, I reject any 'theory' claiming to lead to an 'objective understanding,' but I welcome any 'instrument of intuitive investigation' coming my way. Thus, it is with such premises in mind that I would consider your classification of the four elements of mankind and music with an important correction, though.

"If the first three terms—rhythm, affectivity, and intellect—seem to designate homogeneous elements, the fourth does not. What exactly is 'psychism' in this context? Are impulses, feelings, ideas, and inspirations not 'psychic' phenomena? Does 'psychism' cover all the still unknown elements that do not fit clearly into any of the previous categories? Then, is not 'psychism' close to or even synonymous with the unconscious? But 'unconscious' cannot be a category like rhythm, affectivity, or intellect, since there are rhythmic, affective, even intellectual, unconscious elements notwithstanding that consciousness varies greatly from individual to individual.

"But, if you agree with me that 'psychism' corresponds to various elements, I believe that it would be necessary to find another term. Because classification may have no other purpose than *to bring together what is alike and distinguish it from the other* even 'preventatively,' if I may suggest so. Even if I have no knowledge of the elements of my future discovery, I can foresee the distinct categories to place them without creating confusion.

"What is the fourth element? I do not claim to define its nature, any more than the other three elements. But I know very well that it exists, although the Council of Constantinople (869) denied its presence in man. It is called *the spirit*. Even if I only have a presentiment of power, I have every advantage in not confusing it with that of feeling, nor especially of the intellect, and in foreseeing the mode of its possible manifestation.

"Therefore, 'psychism' dilutes itself: a part of its substance 'rushes,' in the chemical sense, on the affective-sensitive plane; and the other, now freed, reveals itself as 'spirit,' according to its distinct nature. All that is *affective, sensitive, passionate*, finds its musical expression in the science of *harmony* while everything that is *spirit* resides mainly in the *melody*, because *sound* is not the proper musical element. The musical element is what is not heard; it is the spiritual movement foreign to our senses, which we experience while passing from one note to another, and which constitutes the true melody. Therefore, 'melody is the essence of music,' as Mozart put it. And as a harmonist as convincing as Wagner reiterated: "Die einzige Form der Muzik ist die Melodie.' The spirit of man living in his soul, becomes melody. The soul is the passionate place of the manifestations of the spirit, like harmony is the musical support of the melody. The soul can only orient itself according to the spirit, just as harmony, always confusedly affective in its nature, finds its meaning only in melody.

"Regarding the historical applications of your idea, I believe they are possible and very interesting, as long as they are handled with infinite caution. Do you already hear the man in the street who finds the music of Schubert boring under the pretext that it is not 'psychic'? Well, one could say that during the classical period a great synthesis of the four elements took place, under the aegis of the intellect (Bach); that affectivity and intellect have, in the succession of times and places, dissociated and opposed each other to distinguish themselves more clearly, i.e., Schumann as pure affective or Ravel as pure intellectual, or that our time aims at a new synthesis.

"What would the difference between the two syntheses consist of? C. J. Burckhardt said somewhere: 'In Voltaire, rationalism was poetic, even magical. Later, it became flat.' This is true not only of Voltaire, but of all the creative minds of the eighteenth-century rationalism. This is equivalent to saying, I believe, that the intellect then suffers, but *unconsciously*. It is a large part of what I call spirit. No less unconsciously the spirit raise the impulses of romantic affectivity; nowadays, however, the spirit wants to be recognized for itself, in order to preside over the new synthesis.

"But what is the spirit? Rather than launch into an impossible definition, I prefer to suggest that I take this word in a 'religious' sense as the name of the supreme faculty that animates all the others and *connects* man to the divine element from which it comes, and to admit that I recognize its manifestations, its attributes more surely than I can explain its essence. One of the essential characteristics of spiritual consciousness is to be able *to coexist with the act of creation*, which remains forbidden to intellectual consciousness. An example will clarify my point. Take the adagio of the Trio by Gabriel Fauré (please forgive this *idée fixe* of mine): the absolute clarity of consciousness is identified with the supreme creative intensity.

"On another level, Claudel showed himself to be a great artist of the past when he wrote: 'Nothing can be created except in a state of vigilant sleep and of what I will call blind clairvoyance, where *need alone engenders activity*.' While Goethe bore witness to a contemporary or future experience: 'Through a secret psychological orientation, which perhaps deserves to be studied more closely, I believe I have risen to *a mode of production which brings to light, in a fully awakened state of consciousness*, such a page that I still approve of myself today, without perhaps ever being able to swim in this ancient flood.'

"But enough for now. Forgive me for having carried on this far hoping that no one would have misunderstood that I wanted to involve you in a mere quarrel of words. I wanted to make sure that these words express an essential reality."

Notes

1. Reprinted in *I suoni, le onde . . .* Rivista della Fondazione Isabella Scelsi 6 (2001), 11–12.

2. Jean de La Bruyère (1645–1696), French philosopher and moralist, described in his classic *Characters or Manners of the Age*, the mythological figure of Amphion who was said to have built the city of Thebes by the music of his singing accompanied by the lyre.

CHAPTER THREE

~

The Evolution of Harmony

Introductory Note

The Evolution of Harmony and *The Evolution of Rhythm* were conceived probably as a triptych on music aesthetics to be published in various issues of *Suisse contemporaine* beginning with *Sens de la Musique*. The heavily corrected typescripts of *Évolution de l'harmonie* and *Évolution du rythme* show Scelsi's determination to publish aesthetic texts as accurately as possible to avoid, one may think, critical rebuttals from the readership as it had happened with *Sens de la Musique* discussed in the previous pages.

The two *Évolutions* remained unpublished until 1992 when Adriano Cremonese's Italian translation and the original French were issued as two separate monographs not intended for commercial distribution.[1] In his introductory notes, Adriano Cremonese offered some important details regarding the status of the original texts made available to him by Luciano Martinis, Scelsi's literary editor and confidant. Cremonese reported that the text of *Évolution de l'harmonie* consisted of nine typewritten sheets of paper of which only the first five were numbered in progressive order and that a single sheet contained some autographed notes on Debussy, which he (Cremonese) situated between the end of the section on Debussy and the beginning of next argument. The following English translation, however, reports the added section on Debussy in Endnote #4.

Scelsi's Text

Without going back further in probing the evolution of harmony, we may consider Wagner as the most powerful implementer of technical progress in a specific direction—progress that has continued to accelerate ever since at a steady pace. Technically, Wagner's harmony stems from the constant use of chromaticism and the eleventh chord. Now, this chord, which could be considered on one hand as a development of traditional harmony since it adds only a new third to the ninth chord, presents, nonetheless, the peculiarity of possessing a certain bitonality because it results from the aggregate of two chords belonging to different tonalities. It constitutes, then, the first departure from pure tonality within a single chord.

We cannot examine Wagner's ideas or his artistic and philosophical concepts in the present context. His musical *œuvre* and writings offer proofs of how important the cult of race, ancestral blood, his particular mysticism, and so on were for him. Nevertheless, the impulses and psychic images appear to be strongly subordinated or akin to affectivity and to the intellectual element. These elements presented themselves in Wagner's powerful lyricism and majestic structures. The impulses of the psychic and rhythmic order were clearly identifiable through the two still-dominant elements (emotion and intellect), thus appearing mostly in a function conjoined to them. Likewise, the harmonic expression, although tending toward a distinct expression, manifested itself within the framework of a traditional, functional, and tonal harmony. Therefore, this phase of his harmonic evolution appears to correspond perfectly to the parallel phase of evolution of the psychic element in the general balance of the fundamental elements. This is a reason to consider Wagner as the father of modern harmony, because it developed directly and logically from his progressive evolution corresponding to the ever compelling and necessary search for new means of expression.

In the evolution that followed, one cannot ignore the contribution of Russian and Asian music, which both surprised and upset musicians and public just before the beginning of the century. The first provoked reactions as profound as those of Wagnerism because of its rhythmic violence and the splendor of colors and timbre. Thus, it hastened the general evolution in the arts toward the rhythmic and psychic elements. The second provoked above all the study of scales, modes, and rhythms of Asian music, for many—not just musicians—realized that this art had a particular meaning, a different perspective, and that it extended into unknown directions. Since then, these studies and investigations have served Debussy as well as Stravinsky in their conquests and realizations. Also, their art had additional repercussions on the lifestyle and the spirit of the era, and since then different contexts and forms of Asian religions, philosophies, and doctrines became subjects of interest.

Our study is concerned solely with the evolution of harmony in the context of the balance of the fundamental elements in European art and society. This means that African or Asian manifestations are cited or examined here in relation to the contemporary evolution of Western art. The extraordinary rhythmic language of African music or the subtle Asian harmonies in quarter, eight, or sixteenth tones are the result of a particular evolution beyond our control. Similarly, certain characteristics of Russian music show influences the origins of which we cannot trace. African and Asian art taken in their entirety are expressions of rhythmic and psychic characteristics generally endemic to those races. The discovery of this particular mode of expression, at a time when, thanks to its own evolution, the European mind was becoming more and more conscious of the creative power of these elements, indeed, had an overwhelming effect on it and contributed compellingly to the new evolution.

At this moment, we in Europe find ourselves at the beginning of a general orientation that tends ever closer toward a polarization of the rhythmic and psychic elements, as if we were at the beginning of a period of conscious or unconscious research about the means of expression of these elements. "Impressionism, symbolism, poetic realism blend together in one great enthusiasm of curiosity. Painters, poets, and sculptors decomposed matter, paid homage to it, distorted, and re-formed it to bring new nuances and sentiments to words, sounds and colors" (Paul Dukas).[2]

Here are some revealing sentences written by Debussy: "A music truly disengaged from a motif or formed by a single continuous motif that is neither interrupted by anything nor returns to itself. Its development will be no longer consist of material elaborations, this professional rhetoric styled through fine lectures; instead, it will assume a more universal and ultimately psychic dimension."[3]

So, it appears that, among the problems confronting Debussy, the principal one was perhaps the liberation from the still-pervasive formalism which he considered arbitrary from both rhythmic and harmonic points of view.

We do not know what real influence Russian and Asian music had on Debussy. Though there are surely analogies between his whole-tone scale and certain Asian pentatonic scales, it is also certain that he applied procedures stemming from the over augmented chords found in *Tristan* and the harmonic aggregates of the choral writing in *Parsifal*. Furthermore, Debussy did admit having been influenced by the Russians and by Mussorgsky in particular. But what did he ultimately take from Wagner besides the harmonic elements that he developed later, and from the Russians aside from their orchestral refinement of colors and timbres? Moreover, what did the adoption of exotic scales mean besides a conscious or unconscious liberation from traditional harmony while searching for new possibilities for a more immediate expression? On the other hand, all retrospective investigations into probable influences on an artist is in our opinion secondary. The artist's search for personal means of expression runs naturally parallel to the evolution of the new balance of the fundamental elements, which renders it, therefore, necessary. It is natural and understandable that creative artists accept and appropriate all technical means to help them reach their artistic goals; they guard these discoveries and means for what they are, whether they provide answers to the artists' quest for expression or whether they take and use them as a starting point for further transformations and developments. In other words, it is not the "influences" upon the artists that need to be studied but the evolution of the questions that provokes the answers; the "influence" therefore. The importance of "influences" is always related to the degree of accuracy of the answer to a question asked.

In Debussy's days, the general evolution was clear as the rhythmic and psychic elements tended to dominate more and more. This produced an anti-rational, anti-structural reaction. It was only the intellect that lost its supremacy on the artists' aesthetic scale of values, but the intellect was compelled, through new impulses, to adapt to successive formal and rational reconstructions that in turn were quickly rejected, thus becoming outdated.[4]

So, if harmony is still part of a rational order and evolves within the tonal framework, it tends irresistibly to deviate from it. It has become a habit to think of Debussy's music as a revolt against Wagnerism; it would be more exact to say that it was rather a reaction against Classicism intended as formalism conditioned by the intellectual element—and a reaction, also, against Germanic or Italian lyricism as an exuberant expression of affectivity. The music of Debussy was only an anti-Wagnerian reaction insofar as it opposed the two elements that were still all-powerful in this music: intellect and affectivity. It was, in reality, much closer to the Wagnerian sphere than one would think in terms of those elements that would determine all future artistic manifestations. Technically, Debussy's harmony consisted of the following:

1. Superimposed chords of thirds forming a block of double harmonies mostly linked by notes that belong to one tonality or the other.

Double harmonies that could also be considered chords of eleventh, thirteenth, and even fifteenth.
2. Division of the scale in two, three, four, and even six equal parts, the latter division generating the whole-tone scale. That scale already implies a certain atonality because it lacks both dominant and subdominant. This tendency toward atonality also appears in an harmonic passage in which no three successive chords belong to the same tonality, and in the use of chromatic and Asian scales lacking defined tonality.

Thus, on one side there is a creative impulse and images mostly of affective character, but which are so close to the psychic character that they can transform, albeit partially, their particular language; on the other hand, there is still rational harmony, but it leans heavily toward its liberation and already possesses a character of its own. So, we see clearly how the inner evolution of creative forces corresponds exactly to the outer evolution of technique.

Debussy crystallized this phase of human growth so intensely that he—comparable to what Chopin did in his time—fixed it permanently outside his time, and realized totally, therefore, his magnificent destiny as a creator. Before turning to the third phase of harmonic evolution, we reflect on the musicians and their compositions analyzed thus far. We examined more closely the manifestation of evolution in certain composers rather than others because that evolution appears more strikingly and intensely in them, and therefore easier to analyze. Such an evolution, however, is also detectable in Richard Strauss, whose early works possess a very Wagnerian character, both technically and in the balance of the musical elements, that is to say, in their expressed images. Beginning with Wagner through an ever-greater freedom of modulation, unresolved dissonances, and superpositions that are new but always evolving within the framework of functional and tonal harmony, Strauss arrived at the dream of *Elektra*. Here, the Wagnerian material is carried to its final consequences and complexity through the progressive alteration of chords and use of harmonic pedals upon which the crushing of extended harmonies generated a sort of polyharmony and even a sort of atonality. This expression of psychic images was the culmination of Strauss' works. The dominant character of his works became evident in the most intense way conceivable concurrently to his inner evolution as a man at the age of 45. Strauss could not go further. After his masterpieces there were only increasingly light and superficial, even banal expressions, from *Rosenkavalier* to the ballet *Schlagobers* (*Crême fouttée*) to *Arabella*.

The evolution and output of Scriabin are extraordinary. Beginning even before Wagner, because Scriabin's early works up to his Opus 35 often make one think of Chopin, despite a personal stylistic imprint, Scriabin managed, during a short period of time, let us say exactly from Opus 36, written in 1903 to Opus 74 written in 1914, to arrive at some achievements that anticipated those of Alban Berg.

It is difficult to establish how Scriabin's evolution took place. Obviously, one can find in his numerous Preludes for piano elements suggesting Wagnerian chromaticism that are also detectable in successive developments, as well as altered chords of eleventh and thirteenth or even some Debussy derived harmonies. But if one can find all these elements and experimental excursions into extreme harmonics, also pioneered by Debussy— and this last path may have been for Scriabin the most important one to follow—one cannot find a technical evolution that followed logically and progressively. We ought to consider first the inner development of the musician to figure out that this evolution that led him in a short time to the realization of *Prometheus* and the last preludes and sonatas. It is said that Scriabin was fully involved with theosophy, magic, and occultism, and that the second part of his *œuvre* was nothing but an attempt to express religious, metaphysical, esoteric, and even satanic transcendence. In this regard we say that these appreciations of Scriabin's music and ideas are above all the product of ignorance, incomprehension, and traditional hostility from everyone for whom all such research is diabolical. The same can be said regarding the analysis of obscure forces or even present-day exploration of the subconscious and introspection. We think that Scriabin seemed especially preoccupied by certain broad and fundamental ideas, like those of the mystery of creation and the unity of the arts. In his process, he most likely encountered or pursued psychic, religious, or other esoteric experiences, but the idea of total unity haunted him only in order to reach a type of knowledge and a psychic concept of the cosmos. That seems to be what was said in his biography: "Toward the end of his life, Scriabin was engaged in preparing the text for what he named *L'Acte Initial or Mystére* (The Initial Act or Mystery), which should have been performed in India. There, a specially erected hemispherical temple reflected in water would have reproduced the whole globe, the most perfect shape of all."[5]

It remains certain though, that for him the psychic element had clearly become dominant and, consequently, his music was characterized by the harmonic element. Within the space of ten years his various states of conscience or, rather, the imperious need for suitable expressive means of expressions, led Scriabin to an extension of the traditional tonal and harmonic system up to the most recent developments and achievements.

Notes

1. See the monographs *Évolution de l'harmonie* (Evoluzione dell'armonia), hereafter Cremonese 1992a, and *Évolution du rythme* (Evoluzione del ritmo), hereafter Cremonese 1992b. Roma: Fondazione Isabella Scelsi, 1992. These publications contain facsimiles of Scelsi's original typescripts, autographed emendations, and the annotated Italian translations. Cremonese's edition was followed by Kanach 2006 (annotated original French version only), Jaecker 2013 (original French and annotated German translation), and Metzger 2015 (annotated German translation only).

2. Cremonese 1992a, Kanach 2006, and Metzger 2015 do not identify the provenance of the Dukas citation, but Jaecker 2013 proposes the following: "Robert Brussel, Claude Debussy et Paul Dukas," in *La Revue musicale*, Paris, septième année, 1 Mai 1926, 101.

3. Cited in André Fontainas, *Mes Souvenirs du Symbolism* (Paris: Éditions de la Nouvelle Revue Critique, 1928), 92–93. (Cremonese 92a, Kanach 2006, Jaecker 2013, Metzger 2015.)

4. The following notes concerning Debussy were added by Scelsi to the original typescript. He wrote: "After Debussy, there was no descriptive music as that of Beethoven, Liszt, or Wagner insofar that they understood this genre. This is due not only because romanticism was lacking in Debussy, whereas the descriptive musicians were romantic by definition, but rather because, as with contemporary painters, exterior images were no longer represented objectively but were mostly painted and rendered from memory, that is to say, already transformed and charged by psychic elements. These works did not project direct emotions, and even Debussy in his tableaux entitled *Jardin sous la pluie*, *La Mer*, *Nuages* or *Bruyéres* interprets these from the point of view of psychological realism. Chords of ninth, repeated measures, muted strings and brass, and other exterior aspects of his style are similar to the string of pearl-like scales of Mozart, the arpeggios of Schumann, etc.

However, in art, somewhere the accidental shares always some commonalities with the essential. The form is always, according to Remy de Gourmont's utterance, the "formality of essence." In other words, the artist's means of expression have always an indicative value. When Buffon said that "style is man himself," he meant exactly that a thought has only one possible expression and that this expression has the same source as the thought that carries it. The procedures are not style but one of its components, on the other hand though, only those procedures used with systematic constancy become evident to us."

5. According to Cremonese 1992a, and Kanach 2006, this citation was not identifiable, but they affirm that it appeared evident that Scelsi cited from memory as incurred in a double error by modifying the title *Acte préalable* in *Acte Initial* and confusing *Acte préalable* with *Mystére*. Jaecker 2013, 533 added that, "In the summer of 1914 Scriabin wrote down the text to the *Initial Act* . . . and all this taking place in a temple far away in India, in a temple of semi-global shape reflected in water, so as to produce the entire globe—the most perfect of all shapes" (Alfred Julius Swan, *Scriabin*, London: John Lane, 1923, 108–109). Metzger 2015 offers no comments.

CHAPTER FOUR

The Evolution of Rhythm

Introductory Note

In a note accompanying the facsimile of Scelsi's annotated typescript of *Évolution du rythme* (Evoluzione del ritmo) published in Cremonese 1992b, Luciano Martinis wrote that this text was probably written in two different periods.[1] An earlier draft consisted of seven sheets of paper numbered in progressive order, and a second draft comprised seven sheets, typed on the same typewriter as the former but using different paper: the verso of the stationary letterhead available at the *Hôtel de la Paix* in Lausanne. A factor that helps confirming the early 1940s as the time of writing of this and the other essays included in part I of the present collection.

Regarding the content of *Évolution du rythme* (Evoluzione del ritmo), Cremonese observed that the condition of its working sketch and the large section on Stravinsky, in particular, needed corrections, elaborations, and copy editing for an eventual publication which did not occur in Scelsi's lifetime. Thus, one may consider this essay as "unfinished."[2]

Cremonese's decision to publish Scelsi's original material in facsimile in addition to his Italian translation in redacted format was followed by Kanach 2006 and Jaecker 2013 while Metzger 2015 provided only the German translation of the text with commentaries. Some of the endnotes included in the present English translation refer to the above-mentioned scholars' annotations as deemed necessary.

Scelsi's Text

If one can say with certainty that the current harmonic system developed progressively and logically from Wagnerian chromaticism, one cannot, on the other hand, find in Wagner's specific use of rhythm anything that points to the further evolution of this element.

Wagner's most vigorous rhythmic developments, such as those found in the Overture to *The Mastersingers of Nuremberg*, always show a rational constructive order, or they are conjoined to the lyrical impulse which underscores their power. It is rather in the music of Liszt and the third movement of his *Faust Symphony*, in particular, that one finds stunning portentous passages. But it was Russian music that contributed, first and foremost, an expression that was essentially rhythmic; it possessed a basic brutality that was called barbaric, and its power was shocking. At their first performance, the dances from *Prince Igor*, performed with full chorus and orchestra, surpassed in violence everything heard so far. Though rhythm in Borodin's instance was still fully subjected to a structure, it seemed to have already gained an expressive character, a demonstration of something primal, almost physiological, hence its rhythmical physical impact on the audience. This impact increased in power until *The Rite of Spring* and certain compositions inspired by African rhythms. It achieved, therefore, the same degree of intensity in the rhythmic domain as the lyricism of *Tristan* carried in the emotional domain.

We have observed how Debussy was particularly interested in the harmonic elements of Russian and Asian music; their rhythmic significance, however, appeared to have largely escaped him. Yet his reaction against traditional harmony and form led to a relative emancipation of rhythm from the constraints of an academic compositional methodology. Rhythm became more supple, fragmentary, sometimes prone to syncopation. In some sections of his *String Quartet* the rhythmic element had already gained an independent expression. But aside from some exceptions that are mostly symptomatic, Debussy's contribution to the evolution of rhythm would be negligible were it not for the importance of his accomplishments in the emancipation of rhythm from the other elements—primarily from the intellectual—for the realization of its particular possibilities and of its integral manifestation. Some critics discredited Debussy for his want of dynamism, of rhythmic backbone. This dynamism, however, did not wait long to reappear, though it did so in a much different and increased violence! Because the so-called anti-Debussy reaction was, in fact, nothing but the emerging awareness that the rhythmic element was second to harmony in forming the two elements dominating the new balance.

It was with Stravinsky that rhythm manifested itself in all its violence for the first time in European music, should Russian music be considered as such. In fact, if in Stravinsky harmony is essential and significant, rhythm is the determining factor. The evolution and the realization of its full expression are so important and evident in the music of this composer that it warrants examination over the course of his compositions.[3] In *The Firebird*, despite its rhythmic character throughout and apart from certain passages and the entire *Infernal Dance of Kastchei*, rhythm does not appear to be yet separated from the emotional element, which, in turn, is expressed in conjunction with it, thus closely approaching the psychic character. It is true, though, that when rhythm does not appear directly in its characteristic function, it manifests itself abruptly through rapid and quickly exhausted thematic conflicts and interruptions, continuous fractures and metric breaks, constant projection of fragments, and a rapidity of extraordinary and effervescent language. The same happens again in *Petrushka*, namely in the second tableau where rhythm underlines and shares the fragmentation of harmonic expressions giving the sensation of freedom already in its extreme phase and—by now—imminent to total emancipation. One gets the distinct impression of a vital element, which strikes and destroys its chains, lifts mightily one arm then the other, and at every gesture its breathing becomes more powerful and shatters the established order. It is the rhythmic breathing of "Prometheus in chains," a primordial struggle, a dynamic urgency—he, the true giant breaking his last chains appeared among humans, naked, terrifying, and immense. This is the *Rite*! Emotion and intellect are swept away; humans will live their primordial breath, their vital impetus, cosmic . . .[4]

All rhythms have always existed. I do not believe that one can find in Jazz any instance of syncopation, which cannot be found, albeit isolated, in Mozart, Beethoven, or Bach. However, the importance of this syncopation in Jazz is something completely different because instead of appearing sporadically by accident, as a contrasting effect, a sigh in the melodic element or a skip of the heartbeat, it becomes the basis of motion itself, of the whole rhythmic continuity.

The initial rhythmic cell is no longer treated as the dynamic basis for the melodic or structural element, rather it pursues its own particular expression through sequences that obey only its urgency and own laws. Indeed, the exact same thing happened in painting. At about the same time, objects were no longer propped onto a background but were rather conditioned by it, hence the equal importance attributed to both included and excluded spaces. Understood in a similar way, rhythm no longer consists of a series of sounds interspersed with emptiness, but as a series of alternating pauses and sounds, all equal in value. We can even go as far as saying that silences and pauses are linked together by sonorities. This might seem like a dialectic artifice, but it is not so at all. Between sound and silence there is simply a new perspective, comparable to the existing difference between ordinary and stereoscopic photography. Sonorities and silences exist, so to speak, in a three-dimensional space and their relationship is therefore different. In fact, they assume a reality and an entirely new power that once integrated, participate in the rhythmic life of the universe.

As we have said, it is through rhythm that the human being participates in the life of the universe that is vibration, in the life of nature, in the vital élan, and in duration. African and Asian people have a deeper and more immediate consciousness of this than Europeans, for whom rational intellectualism has led to a concept more detached from knowledge. Nowadays, certain scientific works have begun to shed light on the nature of this human participation in the rhythm of the universe. Nevertheless, we are still far from achieving the more intuitive knowledge that African and Asian people have in this domain. Similarly, nothing can even compare yet to the power of the rhythmic language of African music. Without dwelling on what everyone knows about the shattering power of African drumming, we will say that drumming in all its varieties (ritual, musical, and instrumental) must be interpreted and understood as a means of achieving a state of collective consciousness by deregulating one's individual physiological rhythms and their synchronization with some tellurian and universal rhythms. The pauses in this music are [in reality] a portion of space measured by time. Exaltation or euphoria are produced by the sensation of the disruption of one's inner rhythm, that is, of individual and relative time, thus by the sensation caused by the fusion of the being with the flow of cosmic rhythm, in time and duration.

After Stravinsky discovered the true meaning of the rhythmic language, he understood that it was necessary to intensify even more the particular qualities of this element than he had already done in the *Rite*. In that work, in fact, a certain accumulation of means of expression and heterogeneous rhythmic or harmonic procedures, achieved a complexity, which rendered its rhythmic languages at times chaotic despite its outstanding musical power. The different strata did not always subsist fully once superimposed.

Stravinsky composed, therefore, works of smaller scope in which he set out to study a type of rhythmic expression devoid of all other elements, renouncing as a consequence to any harmonic and orchestral showmanship.[5] But those African rhythms, having emerged from vital and elemental rhythms, powerful as they were, fused into a single one; rarely does one find two real rhythms superimposed (when there seem to be more of them, in reality there are only two or even just one, shared among various instruments). Asian music, on the other hand, is comprised in general of several rhythms unfolding on different levels simultaneously, while each one maintains its specific characteristics through a contrapuntal technique of extraordinary subtlety. Hindu, Javanese, and even Arab music, no matter how different one is from the other, all possess the rhythmic consciousness of time like African music.[6]

Compared to much more "frail" music, the brutality produced by the African drums is, so to speak, an acoustical-optical illusion. An Arab or Hindu rhythm, isolated from the others and magnified at will, produces the same effect, but it coexists at times with other [real] rhythms. Furthermore, as we have already observed, the harmonic element is endlessly more developed, including an inter-penetration and absorption of rhythm into duration. The greater complexity of this Indian, Arab music makes it superior to the music of Africa because, when consciousness captures and projects various rhythmic elements, it brings along a more powerful and precise absorption of creative forces. Thanks to this rhythmic multiplicity and its harmonic elements, Asian music seems not only to possess a tellurian character, but possibly an even vaster pulsation. This would explain why, if African music evokes a sensation of panic-like euphoria, Asian music, by contrast, seems not to bear terrestrial characteristics or limits. With its continuous and ethereal dynamism, its inescapable pressing forward, skirting and crossing countless trajectories, the human being's inner time not only seems to be melting into that of nature, of the earth, but it seems, in turn, to becoming one with the absolute cosmic time. Here we are at the threshold of the fourth dimension about which we shall have the opportunity to return later.

The point here is not to examine the musical legacy received and transmitted through Bach. As far as our topic is concerned, we might only point out that of all European musicians, Bach was the only one who possessed a rhythmic dynamism, which although not based on syncopated sequences, miraculously approached an independent, truly rhythmic language. Thanks to his contrapuntal genius, Bach created separations between the levels, which, in turn, created relationships of space and time (that would probably not result otherwise, with an isolated line). It is the attractiveness of this counterpoint that prompted Stravinsky to undertake various experiences and investigations in this direction.[7] But as the use of a European text and preoccupation with a certain architectonical structure had already led in *Les Noces* to a harmony that was somewhat simplified and less psychic [psychological] compared to that of the *Rite* or *Le chant du rossignol*, the growing appeal of the structural element, owing to the intellectual study of

Bach, led Stravinsky imperceptibly to works that were probably outside of his original pursuits. The evolution of the rhythmic and harmonic elements did not manifest itself any longer as clear and affirmative as before; they are no longer Stravinsky's essential means of expression.[8] Since then, Stravinsky's primary preoccupation appeared to have been the reappearance of the structural element, and at times even the melodic motif, whereas harmony tended toward a simplification that, in certain cases, might be considered as regressive insofar as the rhythm even loses the particular character that it had apparently acquired. Therefore, we will let Stravinsky continue his glorious path. Despite the indisputable value of works like *Oedipus Rex*, the *Symphony of Psalms*, and probably those that will follow, it is not very likely that Stravinsky could achieve the same degree of intensity through the intellectual and emotional elements that he mastered in the rhythmic and harmonic domains that dominated his works.[9] He could, however, achieve the above by a total reversal of the balance of the fundamental elements. Therefore, we believe that one can say that if Stravinsky's harmony, like his orchestral timbres and colors, constituted a major contribution toward the evolution of the psychic element, it would be primarily through his rhythmic applications that Stravinsky rebutted Debussy by crystallizing a phase of the evolution of this element, revealing the passage of the elemental and cosmic forces across human consciousness.

The discovery of the real meaning of rhythm affected more or less all musicians. However, only a few comprehended its real significance. Some imitated African rhythms as a topic of folklore; an epidemic of descriptive music, African and Western European, accompanied by ritual or war dances crept into concert programs, not to mention the festivals of American Indian tribes and the entire spectrum of exotic colors. Some of these compositions certainly had a great deal of color and bounce, especially when the dances reflected well the original rhythms and the orchestrations were not travesties better suited for a costume ball. Jazz, on the other hand, seemed to attract a great many musicians. If Stravinsky assimilated its rhythmic, and therefore the essence of Afro-American music, most of the other composers accepted wholesale the autochthonous and original aspects of this music along with the much less interesting and insignificant European imitations. In fact, Jazz is not an African product. One does not find it in Africa; the black people inhabiting the tropical forests do not know it. Musicologists agree that Jazz originated in the Mississippi region. The slaves of families of French origins invented it. The slaves superimposed instinctively the rhythms of their drums on the Europeans tunes they heard, because black people are not inventors of melodies. The rhythmic songs that accompanied the canoe rowers or sometimes the drums have nothing in common with the blues or even with the spirituals. These originated, for sure, in the Gregorian psalm chanting. Both blues and spirituals are as much the work of whites as of blacks, not only because of their contribution of melodic motives but also of their harmonic realizations. In pieces by Ellington, who is perhaps the best African American composer, one finds often even an echo of Debussy. Jazz soon spread through the whole world thanks to the dance fashion. It evolved and quickly became something different than it was at its first appearance. Once commercialized, the result of multiple collaborations and combinations of interests, the melodic themes gradually lost their original quality. Their European provenance becoming more and more easily recognizable and, finally, the best-known melodies and even classical music were downright appropriated and rearranged in Jazz style. So, the "crooners" plague spread worldwide as European tunes were being distorted by whining, saxophone-like voices and syncopated rhythms that became standardized and conventionalized. In reality, most of these serial productions were the product of Westerners, far more appreciated by them than African Americans or Africans. The latter, when practicing among themselves, retreat quickly to less adulterated songs and to more original rhythms. Many European composers did not realize how suspect this dismal exoticism was and whole concertos, even operas emerged with adagios, arias, or recitatives that sounded like blues, and with fox-trot duets and finales. Yet, thanks to the power of the rhythmic language itself, the best of these compositions achieved a real dramatic intensity, especially in the parts where pseudo-African melodic motives disappear, where singing is used rhythmically or consists of open or closed-mouth vocalizations, or used as pedal point with sustained and heartrending tones. These works evoke a rare and often acute sensation of escape in time not on the psychic oneiric level but on our own physical time. When this sensation is joined, without overpowering it, by images of the affective order, it creates a hallucinating atmosphere, a sort of feverish joy or immeasurable despair that seizes the listener. From this viewpoint one may relate or compare *L'Histoire du Soldat* [1918] to the works of Kurt Weill [*Die 3-Groschen-Oper*, 1928], Ernst Křenek [*Jonny spielt auf*, 1926] and others.

Another manifestation of the impact of rhythm on artists resided in their "cult" of the machine and mechanized constructs, a phenomenon common to every art. Here, Futurism was a precursor, for already Marinetti had glorified the locomotive and the chants of pistons and transmission gears in a rhythmic form of onomatopoeic poetry. For the rest, though, Futurism was nothing but the imperious desire for the rhythmic manifestation to come before anything else. It was the result of the irresistible thrust of this element and the people who felt it particularly had to undergo the attraction of the machine and its essential rhythmic drive as the most evident, dominant aspect. Furthermore, this aesthetic of anything mechanic relates to the aesthetic of work, sports, the human effort, and the dynamism of the anonymous masses. Several factors led to this aesthetic, which we shall see when considering poetry. For now, suffice it to say that there is a transposed lyricism in it, because a factory, sport match, or a locomotive are as valuable a subject as a café, a battle, or a horse. Consequently, one should distinguish two categories in the glorification of the machine or its dynamism. The first category uses the machine or the mechanical object in opposition to, and as a substitution for the "landscape," "still life," and so on. The works in this category are based on imitative rhythms and harmonies springing from a desire for reaction or from an anti-sentimental, anti-emotional aesthetic, as much as from the need for a purely rhythmic expression. The proof of this is that the rhythmic language being imitative, like harmony, is not expressed according to its own laws but is subjected to the concept of description outside its model. In other words, it is the depiction of dynamism rather than dynamism itself. Often, works of this category—paintings, symphonic tableaux, and colorful exotic manneristic paintings—suffer from the same shortcomings one finds in photography. Yet, thanks to their true talent and virtuosity, some artists succeed in making remarkable tableaux, some of which are praiseworthy indeed. *Pacific 231*[1923] by Arthur Honegger and *Iron Foundry* [1926–27] by Alexander Mossolov are amongst the best known.

What we have said on the topic of "machine" is equally true about illustrations of the human endeavor or activity. Some works effectively depict games or work. Musically these representations are beguiling, such as *Rugby* (Honegger 1928), *Skating Rink* (Honegger 1922), or *Neues vom Tage* (Hindemith 1929). But here, too, it is not dynamism itself but a depiction, a description of dynamism. Rhythm and harmony are imitative. Both originate from the outer realm and are conditioned by it.

The second category is the one in which the external rhythm of a machine, a game, or human physical motion is developed or expressed subjectively, in ways that artists do not worry at all about process and in which the primal or material origin of rhythm disappears completely. In this case, it is no longer a matter of painting or description, but rather the realization of a rhythm which could belong to a machine, industry, or dancing; its origin is not important. Musicians can feel the real sense of rhythm, to the extent that they free themselves from the subject and its inherent context to achieve a purely rhythmic expression. The establishment of relationships and consonances between human being and the universal dynamism is the primary goal of the rhythmic language. In this case, the role of imitative harmony, if it exists, is completely secondary, like the title of a work which is sometimes suggested to the composer by its rhythmic origin. Such compositions should be named simply "motion" or "rhythm."

The best compositions in this category and those inspired by Jazz constitute, as far as the evolution of rhythm is concerned, authentic realizations and manifestations of this phenomenon. In most cases they express the vital process, from birth to paroxysm or to the death of a rhythm. They could be considered the European interpretation of the African drum, since the Western spirit tends irresistibly, despite everything, toward a delimiting structure. Yet these compositions do not seem to go substantially beyond the point reached by Stravinsky in the finale of *L'Histoire du soldat* or *Les Noces*. At the same time, when several rhythms are treated simultaneously, their individual characteristics seem to dissipate despite the assortment of timbres or registers, which are not always sufficient to obtain or keep the distance between the chosen levels. Consequently, the rhythmic language becomes chaotic in places, though without achieving the power of *The Rite*, if not in some other truly exceptional instances.

Notes

1. Cremonese 1992b, 25.
2. Ibid.
3. Cremonese 1992b, Kanach 2006, Jaecker 2013, and Metzger 2015 quote André Schaeffner's *Strawinsky* (Paris, Les Éditions Rieder, 1931) as the source on Stravinsky consulted and annotated by Scelsi. In fact, all four scholars reproduce Schaeffner's section that aided Scelsi in formulating his assessment of Stravinsky's use of rhythmical patterns and more. Endnote #3 includes the English translation of the paragraphs in Schaeffner's pages 51 and 52, which Scelsi copied down for further examination and eventual insertion in his essay.
4. See Andrè Schaeffner 1931, 51–52, annotated by Scelsi and quoted by Cremonese 1992b, Kanach 2006, Jaecker 2013, and Metzger 2015: "Aside from the prelude and its so far little significant changes of measures, the rhythmic character of *The Rite* is affirmed first and foremost by the [repetitive] chord of the 'Augurs of Spring.' There, as at the beginning and at the conclusion of the 'Dance of the Earth,' the periodic occurrence of the accents is integral to the symmetry of the measures, thus disturbing their interior balance through some syncopations. But the most frequent process in *The Rite* consists of the continuous metrical oscillation: from the 'Sacrificial Dance of the Chosen One,' the introduction of the 9/8 measure provokes a conflict between this measure and the measures in 2/8, 3/8, 4/8, 5/8, 6/8, 7/8 and

12/8. Similarly, the 'Sacral Danse' is constituted by a perpetual alternation between 2/8, 3/8, and 4/8. Finally, the 'Glorification of the Chosen One' proposes fearlessly a series of non-repeated measures such as 9/8 – 5/8 – 7/8 – 3/8 – 2/4 – 7/4 – 3/4 – 7/4 – 3/8 – 2/4 – 7/4 – 3/8 – 5/8 in which the eight note remains the unity of time. It becomes obvious here that Stravinsky confused the rhythmic cell and the metrical cell: the extended range of the measure, of the meter does not exceed that of a figure of a rhythmic fraction thus modifying itself with it: only a common denominator means that there is a basic unity, eight or quarter note, whose meter-rhythms are changing multiples."

5. It was at about this time that Stravinsky assimilated Jazz and African music. [Note by Scelsi quoted in Kanach 2006, fn. 1, 116, Jaecker 2013, fn. 2, 541, and Metzger 2015, fn.4, 21.]

6. At this point a musician will probably have two questions: now that this new-found, liberated rhythmic language is finally understood for what it really means, could one maybe apply it differently than African or Asian people do? And does this rhythmic element necessarily have to be separated from other means of expression in order to preserve its own real expression and characteristics? Stravinsky answers these questions with "Les Noces" and an in-depth study of Bach that led to a number of remarkable works during his neo-classical period. In "Les Noces" he applied rhythmic language to a European text and succeeded in creating a veritable masterwork. [Note by Scelsi citing Schaeffner 1931, 80. It was quoted in Kanach 2006, fn. 1, 117, Jaecker 2013, fn. 1, 545, and Metzger 2015, fn. 6. 23.]

7. This necessity permitted Stravinsky to follow Bach and not the Hindu and the Chinese in spacing the levels. [Note by Scelsi quoted in Kanach 2006, fn. 2, 117, and Jaecker 2013, fn. 2, 545.]

8. At this point, the evolution of rhythm was clearly continued by other musicians. [Note by Scelsi quoted in Kanach 2006, fn. 1, 118, and Jaecker 2013, fn. 3, 545.]

9. To date, the last work we know, *Jeu de Cartes*, composed in 1935–1936, seems to support this assumption. [Note by Scelsi quoted in Kanach 2006, fn. 2, 118, Jaecker 2013, fn. 3, 545, and Metzger 2015, fn. 7, 23.]

CHAPTER FIVE

Art and Satanism

The problem of Satanism in the arts has emerged so often that it deserves consideration as an important matter of consciousness. In fact, this is a problem tormenting, in one form or another, the conscience of all contemporary artists. Thinkers like Maritain[1] and Brémond,[2] writers and critics, have written abundantly on the subject to the point of thinking that art is a true manifestation of the demonic, whether hailing from Baudelaire and Rimbaud, Surrealism, poetry in general, painting, and even music. Let us try, therefore, to summarize the problem.

The first remarks about what type of art fits the definition of demonic or demoniacal are the following:

1. Satanism or Diabolism manifests itself through transfiguration, which lies at the basis of all true poetry. This transfiguration becomes diabolical insofar as it proposes a new and conventional creation of the world since both Satan and the artist possess the ambition to imitate God. The Word was God, and mankind and could not possess, by its very nature, the divine gift. To imitate God and re-create the world, mankind must resort, then, to Satan and not being capable of doing so, must transfigure it.
2. Art is satanic because the work of art is an endeavor against God in the sense that it seeks to upset true values, to replace harmony of nature with artifact harmony, and to find the "truth" beyond God.

3. Art is the faculty of using artificially (by means of processes) real elements by sublimating them through the imagination and the expression of the artist's own beliefs. Artists sacrifice exactitude to their own truth and distance themselves from God insofar as they can transfigure the world. They utter: "It is not a question of imitating nature: art is a second creation which mocks the first; those who claim to imitate God bring ridicule upon themselves. Satan offers us a new path to creation through magic."
4. Satanism manifests itself each time the artist gives up the laws of nature meant for them to follow. It is through the hatred of nature that demonism asserts itself.[3]
5. Satan always wants to mimic God; such is his *raison d'être*. With mankind, the Word cannot secure its creative power. Satan transforms it into magical power. Since his original sin, man turned into a little demon who wanted to mimic God.
6. Art is demonic because of its immorality. There is a certain lack of morality that connotes some works of art, but there is widespread immorality in art simply because it creates a fictitious world as opposed to the true world which is the domain of morality.

If the universe must be viewed as a mirror of God and the poem or painting as a mirror of the universe, nothing prohibits the thought that wanting to equal God—replacing Him by reproducing the universe—constitutes the sin of pride proper to Satan.

On the other hand, let us examine the meaning of "transfiguration" that is supposedly Satan's work. There are several types of "transfigurations," but first, can we negate the poet and the artist to perceive, understand, and realize images or relationships as "transfigured"? Also, it would be necessary to prove that an unusual appearance of nature, due to any schematization, does not cause a reality to be considered as "transfigured." Who can claim knowledge of things as they appear? Appearances change as one probes them and even more so by getting closer to the true "knowledge" of the essence of things.

Artists working in two dimensions transfigure nature in the eyes of people who perceive the third dimension; but is not knowing the perspective a diabolic stylistic influence? Are those artists who try nowadays to introduce the fourth dimension diabolically transfiguring nature? Or is theirs a justified search for what nature is? Furthermore, is not nature itself in a perpetual phase of "becoming"? Should nature be always reproduced in a static manner when it is not so even for a fleeting moment in the eye of the painter and the poet? Can we not reproduce nature in its "becoming"? Why consider "transfiguration" the only representation of reality seen in a different way? To imitate nature *in sua operazione*, in its very unfolding in permanent creations, is it not to transfigure it? On the contrary, it is an even greater approximation of reality, because nothing is static, thus a static reproduction is incorrect. Let us discuss, then, whether there is real transfiguration.

There are indeed cases of real transfiguration. Baudelaire stated that "the dispersion and the focusing of the self: those two movements are of the essence."[4] The cases observed above belong to the focusing of the self, that is, a state of consciousness resulting from a polarization geared toward the faculties of intellectual knowledge, the establishing of relationships, identification, and so on. Dispersion, on the other hand, extends from romantic inspiration to surrealist automatism, visionary, and ecstatic states of mind whether artificially induced or not.

Now, it would be necessary to prove that all creative states of inspiration or exaltation are diabolical; or that to put oneself intentionally in a state of dispersion would be to succumbing to the will of the devil.

It is obvious that sheep and angels enter through an open gate, as well as wolves and unicorns; but, often, such invasions, when not specifically called for are at least desired by the artist. Either action—the dispersion and focusing of the self—is determined by the unconscious or subconscious of the well experienced creative artist. In other words, dispersion is not a diabolical state because it can benefit a very high level of inspiration or mediation; but evidently, given the human nature, the danger of the appearance of lower and even very low elements is quite great. However, this does not imply, we repeat, that the transfigurations due to subconscious images, oneiric visions, hallucinations, hypnotic, or automatic states must be imputed to Satan. In fact, these are particular psychic states of mind through which artists sometimes obtain either a disturbance of their sensitivity—and therefore a new order of perception—or a refinement of it and a more subtle perception of exterior or interior experiences, or still a flood of inner experiences forbidden in different states of consciousness, or in a state of complete passivity—an impersonality which puts them in contact with supernatural forces or entities. So, it does not seem that Satan is responsible, either for the manifestations of focusing of the self nor for those of dispersion, especially since creative artists whether belonging to one class or another due to their temperament or aesthetic conceptions, can nevertheless shift from one method to another.

The artistic vocation is a particular activity for some. Artists are not devilish. They are born endowed with certain psychophysical abilities, perhaps due to genes, and they express their creative activity because it is their nature.

Like all people, artists can fall under the diabolical influence by wishing evil rather than good, turn to darkness instead of light; the result is a satanic activity, but not more than any other human activity. Artistic creation is a completely natural activity and not *a priori* a diabolical one, because genes or psychophysical characteristics are hereditary or the result of circumstances. It would be quite difficult to claim that such a gene is not diabolical except when it reaches the creative artists when in combination with other activities. Then, it could result in a demonic activity. Let us discuss now the immorality factor.

Art is a system in conflict with the natural harmony of things. The harmony of things is a harmony of utility; art is immoral because it is useless. In fact, as Remy de Gourmont said: "If art is given a moral purpose, it would no longer be useless." [5] A concept we should ponder about it. First, the harmony of the useful involves an order of necessity which generates such a harmony. But what about disorder, does it exist? Bergson has shown in his *L'Evolution créatrice* (1907) [*Creative Evolution* (1911)] that "disorder" was only apparent and reacted to a different order than the one under consideration.[6]

Mankind is capable of uselessness and even gratuitous acts. Moreover, people forged a host of worldly habits, patriotic obligations, and sports which have no relationship between necessity and their cognitive faculties, which is perhaps a good thing should one formulate an idea of nature that does not correspond to reality. Uselessness, if it ever existed, is the generator of other values like the act of dancing which would only begin when the legs move uselessly. It would happen when prose sacrifices logical reasoning and rhetorical power to transform itself into a poem. The abandonment of the order of the useful not only gives rise to aesthetic values and to a different order: one must also think about its correspondence to that part of uselessness of which people are capable of solely because it is embedded in them.

Who can judge the usefulness of actions of necessity and, ultimately, whether usefulness itself may lead beyond usefulness from an absolute point of view? Who can prove that the "magical" part of a useless activity, like dancing or any artistic creation, may not be more useful and active according to a plan as preestablished of the natural order of necessity? Would it then be a useful activity? Why limit an *a priori* reason for useful Godly activities and consider all others as demonic, when they more likely fulfill an equally useful role on another level? Why does the role of this creation—which I call "super-utilitarian"—fail some people almost from birth while it fails others during the process of utilitarianizing? Some are, therefore, made for creating and bringing order to the harmony of necessity, others to the harmony of useless or super-useful. Such is the role of the artist. Still, it is possible, in addition, that the crystallization of powers manifesting themselves in art has a real utility of a psychic order, without taking into account the theories according to which certain powers or ideas accumulate and incarnate in some people who, in turn, function as a liberating power transferred onto the collective soul seen as an entity, a single body, and so on. Another accusatory factor purports that art is satanical and immoral because it creates a fictitious world in opposition to the real world, the domain of morality, thus putting into play the concepts of reality and fiction.

If art is the manifestation of states of consciousness and images of the artist, should these states or images be considered as fiction or as reality? One can very well assume that the work of art is the manifestation of an inner reality, and that the world of fiction is a world just as real. In fact, what makes a "real" world real? Everyone knows that our senses do not transmit the absolute reality of things, their essence, but a limited, subjective impression. The real world is impossible for us to perceive, neither in its essence nor in its development. Why then do we insist on contrasting the unprecise words "real" and "fiction," the latter being closer to reality than the former? So, let us put aside such a comparison as well as the other concerning the concepts of morality and immorality to which they are sometimes linked.

One more negative factor: The arts are satanical because God calls on mankind to discern good from evil, beauty from ugliness, according to a canon valid for all. But the consciousness of the artist resolves a new problem of good and evil before each work of art. Artists are the absolute masters of the world they create and for doing that, they must sacrifice morality and find, despite themselves, the strength to figure out the universe.

We have already observed that it is a question of the morality of the useful, that is to say, the harmony of necessity. Art does not sacrifice this, but it juxtaposes itself to another harmony. We have thought about "transfiguration" and how, in most cases, it is not a question of transfiguration but of reality. Morality, therefore, rests in the good and evil dichotomy and "transfiguration," when it comes to dispersion and the manifestations of evil or dark forces.

So, it seems to me that we are talking about art and the mankind factor: the work of art capable of including, like any other endeavor, a dose of evil which may not be necessarily *evil*.

Moving forward, I say that European Christian or secular morality is not identical to those predicated and practiced by other religions in other times or countries; I cannot say, for instance, that other moralities exist without being satanical. I say, however, that artistic activity belongs to any time and place. It is true that Plato clearly detected the calamity of poetry and music. He was not fond of the former and would have liked to suppress all "modes" of the latter except the Ionic and the Dorian because, in the elaboration of his morality, he feared the appearance of aesthetic or artistic elements which would have risked being misunderstood.

There have always been some kind of "forbidden" music and art from the Chinese to present times, to say nothing of what the whole world knows, namely those artistic manifestations forbidden because they do not conform to certain social ideas espoused by governments that consider art only from political and propagandistic points of view.

The truth is that art transcends the human idea of morality far exceeding any current or philosophical doctrine and can never be considered moral or immoral as a creative activity and a *phenomenon of creation* (unless mankind indulges knowingly in the pursuit of evil).

When Baudelaire or Rimbaud invoke Satan, they seek imagined emotions they call demoniacal, and which, therefore, stimulate an aspect of their particular nature.

Artists can very well open the gates of their consciousness to the invasion of more or less dark forces, and consciously invite the devil to their aid; but, in most cases, they only adorn certain particular psychological states with demonism. Such action causes only balances or imbalances of consciousness and sensibility. Thus, they appear to the artists as different experiences or in different and more subtle forms.

There is really no need to invoke the devil. Decentralization (dispersion) as well as centralization (focusing of the self) directed to the point of hallucination are states of conscience in which Satan can intervene at will or if he is called upon, but which in no way are diabolical in themselves and can very well exist without his intervention. Besides, should it be necessary to side with Satan one could side with the Angel as well.

Satan's presence is clear in Baudelaire when he states that "in man there are two simultaneous postulations, one toward God, the other toward Satan," and Rimbaud: "Me! I who called myself a magus or an angel!" or Mallarmè in *Les Fenêtres*: "I admire myself and see an angel!" Sometimes angel, sometimes demon, or both at the same time, is really only to adorn these attributes with certain particular states of consciousness resulting from a polarization toward the search of knowledge—a search in which everyone in a way suffered or sought more or less voluntary psychic experiences. Often one can even believe that they wish to be alternately angel or devil for the same cause—the same goal, the same search. They engage in one or another state of consciousness which is out of their balance, and which allowed them to seek experiences in the domain of the knowledge of the absolute.

Thus, it is that this search for knowledge or the absolute is ultimately felt as demoniacal or angelic by the artists themselves or considered as such by certain critics.

Art is satanical because it seeks on its own merit the knowledge given either by the grace of God or by a disposition of mind auspicious to Him.

Now, it seems to me that this search for knowledge is innate to every evolved human being. The philosophy of Plato, Descartes, or Bergson, the mystic experiences of St. John of the Cross, Novalis, and Swedenborg among others, are replete with challenges—or initiations if you prefer— which force the natural souls to reach the knowledge of the Supernatural through various paths. Art is an instrument of an *a priori* perception of essences, a means of intuitive communication with the powers of the Beyond.

Artists search their inner selves deeply to apprehend the ultimate reality hiding behind the appearance of things. Can we ask art, as some people have, to renounce its metaphysical function? This act of transcendence is born to it, because its very role is to transgress the laws of the universe by crystallizing a moment of becoming, casting it into a lasting form. Art only has real value when it collects some miraculous parcels of the inaccessible Absolute.

At this point, artists find themselves in the grip of dangerous temptations and in a spiritually perilous situation; but great art needs this spiritual and mystical knowledge despite the dangers that accompany it—and moreover, artists may well be prepared to succeed "this attempt to experience the state of grace," as Daniel Rops very aptly put it, we believe that God will forgive the possible sin of pride of the artists, because they are the ones called upon to quest for the Absolute.[7]

Notes

1. Jacques Maritain (1882–1973), French philosopher and one the principal interpreter of Thomism. [Kanach 2006, fn. 2, 219, and Jaecker 2013, fn. 1, 575.]

2. Henri Brémond (1865–1933), French critic and historian, author of the monumental *Histoire littéraire du sentiment religieux en France*, among other texts. [Kanach 2006, fn. 3, 219, and Jaecker 2013, fn. 2, 575.]

3. See the note by Scelsi quoted in Kanach 2006, fn. 1, 222, and Jaecker 2013, fn. 1, 577. He wrote: "Baudelaire was a demoniacal type. He was the first to have the

courage to hate nature. In order to demonstrate the weakness of natural harmonies and the superiority of the imagination, Baudelaire compares nature to a dictionary. A dictionary is harmonious in the sense that it is ruled by order (which we could take for divine because it has been imposed). But the poet does not agree with the dictionary; he searches it for elements of his thought but orders them according to his own fantasy. He jumps up because of theories that want to make art into a copy of nature: 'Who would dare to assign art the sterile function of copying nature?' For him art is a weapon that the devil has given him to "combat" nature.

"He says, there is no artwork without the devil's participation. Rimbaud's diabolism is affirmed by his position of rejecting nature. This rejection is, first of all, translated into a poetics in which he puts his entire will to work on deregulation. The disorder of his phrases is only a procedure for making us seize another truth than that of nature; through this disfigurement he achieves poetry: 'In the end I find the disorder of my mind sacred.' He puts forward a real re-education of the senses in a systematic way: 'I got used to simple hallucinations; I saw very clearly a mosque on the spot of a factory, a salon on the bottom of a lake' and so on.

"Mallarmé is possessed from the demon of analogy. Analogy is at the basis of all occult science. The poetic universe does not move anymore along the lines of logic but of analogy. Mallarmé understands analogy as recreating a world. Through the demon of the precious artifice, Mallarmé makes for himself a new world, like any poet."

4. "De la vaporization et de la centralization du *moi*. Tout est là." See *Mon coeur mis à nu*, in *Oeuvres completes*, tome II, Paris, Gallimard, "La Pléiade," 1975, 676. [Kanach 2006, fn. 1, 224, and Jaecker 2013, fn. 2, 578.]

5. "*Si l'on donne à l'art un but moral, il cesse d'être puisqu'il cesse d'être inutile.*" Remy de Gourmond (1858–1915), French writer who dedicated part of his work to the symbolism of opposition between the soul and the body. [Kanach 2006, fn. 1, 225, and Jaecker 2013, fn. 3, 583.]

6. Henry Bergson (1859–1941), *L'Evolution créatrice* (Paris: Alcan, 1907), "*De la signification de la vie. L'ordre de la nature et la forme de l'intelligence*," in Oeuvres, Paris, Presses universitaires de France, 1959, 653–725. [Kanach 2006, fn. 2, 225, and Jaecker 2013, fn. 4, 583.]

7. Citation not identified in Kanach 2006, fn. 1 230. However, according to Jaecker 2013, fn. 1, 591, Scelsi paraphrased a quote by Henri Daniel-Rops [Henri Petiot] (1901–1965) taken from an essay by Swiss writer and critic Marc Eigeldingen (1917–1991) on poetic angelic beings. He wrote: "Poetry is in a way a learned incarnation of Grace, 'an attempt to give a profane expression of the state of grace,' according to the excellent formula of Daniel-Rops" (*De la poésie comme exercise spiritual*, Fontaine 19–20, March–April 1942). See Marc Eigeldinger, "Petit traité de l'angélisme poétique," in *Suisse contemporaine*, No. 1, Lausanne: Concorde. Janvier 1944, 26. This is the same issue of *Suisse contemporaine* in which Scelsi's essay *Sens de la musique* was published next to Eigeldinger's essay. In his essay, the Swiss writer and critic quoted authors such as Baudelaire, Rimbaud, Mallarmè, or Max Jacob, with whom Scelsi was familiar.

CHAPTER SIX

Unity and Equality of the Arts

I

For centuries, the unity of the arts has been subject of innumerable reflections, studies, and essays. Certain artists and theoreticians have probed the laws of matter, recognized similarities, discovered their concordances, and attempted daring scientific parallelisms, syntheses, or tentative comparisons. Others, on the contrary, approached this "unity" subjectively by applying different methodologies such as association or transference of organic sensations and images, or the possibility of future expressions in one art or another born out of the same states of consciousness and leading to parallel technical research.

It seems useless at this juncture to cite examples whose list could be endless. Everyone is familiar with the most recent thoughts on these subjects and the "discoveries" of Baudelaire, Gautier, Rimbaud with his famous sonnet, as well as Scriabin with his *Prometheus* enriched by color projections, or some grandiose works based on the synthesis of all the arts, each represented in a sort of gigantic counterpoint supported by the expertise of numerous "painters of sonorous vibrations or instrumental timbres," not to mention, scent emanating from pipe organs and the exploits of certain cinematographic extravagances. These problematics have been approached sometimes empirically in a subjective manner and sometimes rationally by the followers of scientific or pseudoscientific objectivism.

Research or experiments in this area can be divided into two categories:

1. The first category includes research and experiments belonging to the scientific domain, which are based, therefore, on the study of matter and its laws. In fact, one can establish relationships between the vibrations of sound and colors, scents, heat, and so on. One could—should the need arise—establish through mathematical calculation the relationships between these vibrations and recognize, for example, the proportions existing between a sound and its harmonics or a color and its properties. Thus, it is possible to think of these concordances theoretically, admitting the existence of their unity and recognizing it scientifically. Experiments attempted in this direction have, however, nothing in common with artistic expression. Indeed, if a well-trained ear can detect the harmonics of a note—already a quasi-impossibility in a single or a series of chords and if a sensitive eye can perceive color properties, it is impossible for the human sensory apparatus to feel the correspondences between the vibrations of sound, color, or scent, much less the secondary correspondence like those between harmonics and color properties. Moreover, similar relationships can be detected in sculpture and poetry. Now, a poem exists independently of the voice that utters it, the precise calculation of the vibrations emanating from vowels and consonants, and yet one does not get any nearer to the very substance of the poem. It would be necessary, then, to calculate the vibrations produced by the images and the thoughts of consciousness, which may be possible someday, and to establish relationships between the vibrations of sound, colors, and at one point even between those of life itself: the concept of the Whole to the absolute unity in the form of energy or vibration. It is possible that one day the human brain will discover the laws of the cosmos, but it must be said that in any case these laws and relationships will remain purely speculative and intellectual.
2. Regarding the second category of experiments, which includes those of the artists who sincerely believe they are the receivers of certain messages through exceptional neurological connections, we may remind them that one sensorial event sometimes awakens another!

    Certain drugs such as opium or hashish also stimulate or establish sensorial connections. The correspondences felt, therefore, can only be occasional and of a purely personal and empirical order. It is also true that auditory sensations can awaken sensations of hearing and tasting, or vice versa, either immediately or after a delay; but this phenomenon is the result of uncontrollable correlations like those occurring between affective and psychic images.

According to the most recent studies and research on automatism, the innate language, or the creative forces which we have described as the basic elements, seem to flow continuously through the human body creating in their consciousness a flux of vibrations of which only a minimal part is recognized and identified by the sensorial, intellectual, emotional, or psychic memory in the form of images, sensations, concepts, and states of consciousness. We do not know to what extent this flux can keep its creative power without interruption. Probably not at an identifiable variable speed and intensity which is registered by the subconscious and so has escaped any form of detection by the psycho-physiological organism. It is true, therefore, that one can think of the vibrations produced in the consciousness by thought or image which emerge to the fore stimulated by consonances and resonances of other images stored in the subconscious. These correspondences though, once created or felt, can also be occasional and belong to a subjective order as they cannot be established rationally. Moreover, the associations or resonances thus produced can be considered as the secondary effect of unknown laws whose intensity is, except in special cases, necessarily reduced to that of the primary image.

Artists are mistaken when they adhere to the idea of the subjective fundamental unity of art by systematically provoking these associations or secondary resonances to achieve means of expression pertaining to the pursuit of a different type of art. The path they follow is, therefore, misdirected and uncertain.

As we observed at the beginning, to seek affinities, concordances, and the unity of the arts by considering only material factors through the calculation of vibrations, proportionality, the golden ratio, or any other means and measure is the equivalent of seeking the unity of the arts in the scientific realm. Moreover, a similar search undertaken by following the surging analogies or correspondences commonly found in the psyche is the equivalent of searching for the unity of the arts at the opposite pole, absolute subjectivism. In both cases, this type of research leads to erroneous aesthetic theories.

Current scientific knowledge of the physical laws of sound or plastic matter goes far beyond traditional and scholastic concepts. Their applications constitute an enrichment of the means of expression. Regarding sound or plastic matter, we will observe in the pages ahead how the same progression is accomplished in all the arts and the same scientific laws are applied, consciously or not, in the evolution of technology resulting—one should keep in mind—in a subjective evolution, the necessary means for its projection as a parallel expression.

We cannot follow, therefore, certain theorists who wish to see in music only a system of sound waves and, consequently, advocate for a musical art based solely on laws inherent to these energies resulting from calculations, which would amount to considering art as a total entity and not as a projection of consciousness. We can no longer admit and consider cognition as a sole element to the exclusion of the others, a move that appears unjustified nowadays given the relative balance of the fundamental elements. Music, which is not subjected to the intellectual filter, does not identify itself with the images generated by the fundamental forces, although it constitutes a part—perhaps the greatest part if not the very meaning of such images. In other words, music has no need for the illuminating aspect of the intellect, which identifies reality only through representations. The word "image" in relation to music may seem to contradict what has been said above, although only a portion of the images created in a continuous stream by the forces of the fundamental elements is identified. Likewise, the unidentified images, meaning the virtual ones, create states of consciousness. They appear similar in nature and can shift unpredictably from the unknown to the known realm of consciousness.

Different arts are only different means of expression through which vital impulses are exteriorized while keeping their common laws in each of their particular expressions. It is the identity of these laws in their various manifestations that constitutes and establishes the fundamental unity of the arts.

II

If a false interpretation of fundamental unity can lead some artists to succumb to aesthetical errors, others are prone to proclaim the supremacy of one art over another. Surprisingly, we find statements of such nature issued by individuals who are rightly considered to have analyzed with subtlety and depth the writings and thoughts of the greatest scholars dealing with artistic problems.

Here is, to cite an example, Mallarmé's opinion, which according to Pierre Beausire, considered poetry as humanity's highest and most complete accomplishment, one that justified its presence in the universe and, simultaneously, the universe's own existence. Beausire wrote:

> Superior to the philosopher, as any creator of values is to those who appreciate them; as the spirit that attempts to set ablaze, in a moment of consciousness, the whole of the inseparable multiplicity of the Real, is to the spirit that conceptualizes and forges from it the rational whose demand for coherence materializes only after the fact as if it were the being's logical constitutive unity. Superior to the painter or the sculptor who localizes the complex details

of the emotion or the vision in an order of determined its variants. Superior to the musician who only materializes the power of our instinctive impulses and the shape of our fundamental dynamism by abolishing the distinct voice of our consciousness. It is the poet who thrives, finally, in the immediacy of life "singing" its praises that let us grasp its innermost law thanks to the language he uses.[1]

Mallarmé owes this conception of a universal aesthetic to his great idea of the word that places poetry at the top of the hierarchy of values. But here is what Wagner wrote about it:

In order to advance toward the divine, music, unlike the other arts, need not to pass through the objects of the intellect and its efforts. In fact, once the intellect [cognition] is disregarded, music lives directly in infinity and in life through its rhythm, melody, and harmony. It is true that all arts and especially poetry must pass through the objects of the intellect without harming the life of art; on the contrary, it can be useful to it, insofar and only, if their forms are finite [completed] in the infinite flux. Few are those who, by such assertion of the finite, succeed in attaining the eternal life of God. It is certain, though, that these reach the highest spheres through any form of art and yet it is equally clear that the others remain inevitably linked to the finite they invoke. The difficulty of raising an object to the level of Idea through contemplation does not exist for the musician since music itself is the *Weltidee*, the Idea of the World (Wagner uses the word "idea" in the Platonic sense) [note by Scelsi], by which it manifests its essence immediately, while in the others the limitation of the individual Will is caused by the illusion of his difference and separation from the essence of things—an illusion that man can only free himself through disinterested and impersonal contemplation; on the other hand, the Will feels immediately united beyond any limit of individuality, because it is through the opening of the gate that the world enters into it— and it into the world. In music, the outer world communicates what we call out from our depths through our ears. The complete break of all limits of appearance must inevitably evoke an exaltation in the musician that is incomparable to any other, for he feels he is re-embodying the essence of the world which he can expresses beyond all rationality or intuition. Only one condition may be superior to his, that of the saint, for it is not subject to disturbances, while the musician's clairvoyant exaltation alternates with periods of return to the condition of individual Will. In truth, music is to the other arts what religion is to the church.[2]

Gauguin expressed his thoughts about painting in a quite concise way when he said:

"Painting is the finest of all arts; it sums up every sensation in it because the artist can create a story at a single glance and have the soul overwhelmed by the deepest memories without any effort of memory, all is represented in a single moment."

And Rodin on behalf of sculpture . . .[3]

There is no need here to examine at length the ideas of Mallarmé, Wagner, Gauguin, and others. They appear correct to us for what the analytical aspect of the various artistic expressions is concerned, and erroneous from the comparative side of things. To pursue this discussion further, we would have to revisit and reconsider the much studied and controversial problem of the limits of language and the inability of words to define anything if not by approximation or evocation of images already established. The same can be said regarding the question of the relationships between the visual arts' static quality and duration, and so on. In a nutshell, here rests the whole problem of the relative communicability of artistic expression, not to mention the universality of the arts. But all these considerations, which would require volumes to sort out, exist only in relation to the reader, the viewer or the listener in their actions and eventual reactions to others. The very essence of the artistic creation, the real substance of the work of art is not being questioned here. All artistic expressions are the product of the same elements. Their essence is one and the same. The greater or lesser resonance and action of an art form in relation to specific purposes or applications has nothing to do with their value. The same can be said about their greater or lesser appreciation, as well as the understanding by the public at large according to their culture. Paying particular attention to a given country or historical period is not a proof of the superiority of one mean of artistic expression over another. At most, it proves the existence of a momentary greater receptive sensitivity for one form of expression over another on the part of an individual, group, or collectivity. This sensitivity is not, though, the very subtle and decisive prerogative of the creative artist only, but it exists in everyone to different degrees, because sensitivity includes all psycho-physiological perceptive possibilities in possession of mankind. It is, therefore, the extreme subtlety of one or more of these means that distinguishes a painter from a poet or a musician. Indeed, each of these means of perception can be considered a registering device, a revealer, or even a filter, an analyzer, to use a scientific terminology. Depending on their nature, these devices or filters generate a ledger, the revelation of the fundamental forces in one form or another. In mankind, one or more of these perceptual *apparati* are normally more developed, sensitive, and subtle than others, thus determining a vision of particular enlightenment. Human beings register the vibrations of matter through their organic and sensorial disposition, and those of emotional, psychic, or spiritual order through the psychic side, thus uniting the two poles of the forces passing through consciousness and subconscious.

Just as the difference between matter and spirit is not of a substantial order but only a question of intensity or thickness, so there is only a difference of that order between perceptual elements belonging to sensorial sensibility and those of emotional or psychic sensitivity. Human beings possess in their sensibility perceptual *apparati* of different intensity or thickness corresponding to the whole range that unites the pole of vibrations of matter to that of the spirit.

We have previously identified four fundamental elements: rhythm, affectivity, intellect, and psyche as different manifestations of energy at the core of universal unity.

Just as we can analyze these elements separately, although there is no separation or dissolution of continuity between them, we can recognize in human sensibility the distinct means of perception, although they all interact with one another.

As a reminder, here are the four degrees—each corresponding to a fundamental element:

1. Biological or rhythmic memory by which the functioning organs receive and take certain positions, certain imprints, and keep them sometimes indefinitely.
2. Emotional memory resulting from the repetition or intensity of certain emotional reactions.
3. Mental memory in which all that is known and identified by the intellect is inscribed and retained by it.
4. Psychic memory, which registers all that is forgotten or not retained by the biological, emotional, and mental memory, as well as all images of a rhythmic, emotional, and mental order not identifiable by the intellect; and finally, the prenatal or hereditary element.

Regarding the aural sensibility, one can recognize also the following four degrees:

1. Pure physiological hearing, that is to say, the perception of sounds or physical noises.
2. Emotional hearing, which perceives the relationship between rhythms, intensity, pitch, and timbre of two or more intersecting sounds.

3. Psychic hearing which perceives the analogies and relationships between each sound in aggregate or harmonic combination.
4. Intellectual hearing which perceives and recognizes the physical and formal relationships between sounds identified by signs or names.

Conclusion

It is evident then, if degrees of sensitivity or perfection exist even for the constitution and functional faculties of the sensory organs like eye or ear and their sense of greater or lesser perception, it is more so for the nonphysical and more subtle elements of sensibility. It would appear, therefore, that each human organ of sensory perception corresponds to an emotional, mental, and psychic apparatus of perception whose sensitive ability to perceive and record is incomparably greater than those of the sensorial sensitivity. So, if the eye of a painter, the ear of a musician seems to perceive and hear more things, more relationships if not all things according to visual and sound images, even more so will the most subtle elements of sensibility register multiple elements in their own particular way arriving then at the point of revealing, identifying, and determining, mainly, in one form or another, a greater or lesser part of the flux of creative vibrations which cross the artist's consciousness. But a filter, an illumination is not by its nature superior to another. The lens of a telescope which allows the exploration of the universe is not superior to the lens of the microscope which allows the investigation of the infinitesimal. It is only the quality of the lens and its power that can possibly be subject to comparison, and that in a still quite relative way, not their very nature. One can claim even less when establishing superiority based on the appearance, the revelation of the nature of things, plants, or atoms. The identification of different forms exists only through the limitation of our sensory, cognitive, and affective sensitivity. If we can admit that sometimes our psychism escapes this illusion, thus giving us an exceptional feeling of fullness, this state may be understood as part of super-normal phenomena, as all human beings' perpetual possibilities cannot register, feel, identify, or recognize only an imperfect part of the creative energy that passes through them.

Intellectual images, plastic, or sound are only particular appearance of the various energies that manifest themselves in the cosmic unity.

Notes

1. Sharon Kanach thinks "without a doubt" that the text of *Unité et égalité des arts*, was written by Scelsi in the early 1940s for a public talk. (Kanach 2006, fn. 1, 231.)

2. As the source of this quotation, Kanach 2006 proposes *Gloses* de Pierre Beausire (1902–1990). Paris, Librairie Honoré Champion, 1974. Jaecker 2013, on the other hand, lists Beausire's *Essai sur la poèsie et la poetique de Mallarmè* (Lausanne: Roth, 1942), 210 as the text that Scelsi most likely consulted.

3. Since Scelsi quoted Wagner from memory without identifying his sources, we propose the following reference: "Such an object which is by pure contemplation to be elevated to Idea does not present itself to the musician; for his music is in itself an idea of the world in which the world directly presents its nature, while in other arts is presented only through the intermediary of cognition. This can only be understood as the *individual* Will (reduced to silence in the visual artist by pure contemplation) being awakened in the musician as *universal* Will and as such being well and truly recognized itself, over and above all contemplation, as self-conscious. Hence the very differing circumstances of the creative musician and the designing artist; hence the fundamentally different effect of music and painting. Here a sense of deep calm; there the highest stimulation of the Will caught up in the individual as well as in the delusion that it is distinct from the nature of things outside himself, a Will which transcends its boundaries only in pure disinterested contemplation of objects. On the other hand, the Will of the musician at once feels itself united above all bounds of individuality: for hearing opens the gate through which the world comes to him and he to it. This breaking down of all boundaries of appearance must necessarily evoke in the inspired musician an incomparable sense of rapture. In this rapture the Will recognizes itself as all powerful: it does not have silently to refrain from observation, but it proclaims itself aloud as a conscious idea of the world. Only *one* state can surpass his: that of the saint, especially since his circumstances are constant and imperturbable, whereas the musician's rapturous vision has to alternate with the constantly returning state of his individual consciousness; and we must consider this state the more wretched in that his enthusiasm has raised him higher above all boundaries of individuality. The sufferings with which the musician has to pay for the enthusiasm which so captivates us, may make claim, indeed, to sainthood. For his art truly relates to the complex of the other arts as does religion to the church." See Allen, Roger, *Richard Wagner's Beethoven (1870): A New Translation* (Woodbridge: Boydell & Brewer, 2014), 61–63.

4. Scelsi's quotation from Rodin was evidently jotted down on a loose sheet of paper that has not been found.

CHAPTER SEVEN

Epilogue

Rome 1945–1950

Giacinto Scelsi and his wife, Dorothy Ramsden, returned to Rome in 1945. The couple separated when Dorothy decided to move permanently to England for "patriotic reasons," she told her daughter Katie (Caterina Imperiali di Francavilla), who also moved permanently to England in 1946.[1] Scelsi and Dorothy divorced in Switzerland in the spring of 1948.

In Rome, Scelsi and his mother, donna Giovanna d'Ayala Valva, initiated a project dedicated to the publication and performance of the music that Scelsi composed in Lausanne in the early 1940s and elsewhere in the 1930s. Edizioni De Santis, a small but well-reputed Roman publishing concern, was contracted to issue a catalogue of works representative of the composer's talent.[2]

The catalogue included the following compositions, which were edited for publication probably by Vieri Tosatti, Mario Zafred, and perhaps Roman Vlad:

1947—*12 Preludi* per pianoforte (prima series), 1936–1940
Sonata per pianoforte (1940–1942)
Variazioni e Fuga per pianoforte (1940–1943)
Sonata per violino e pianoforte (1934)
Quattro Poemi per pianoforte (1934–1937)
Capriccio per pianoforte (1935)
Trio per violino, violoncello e pianoforte (1939)
Ballata per violoncello e pianoforte (1943–1944)

1948—*Quartetto* per due violini, viola e violoncello (1942–1944)
Dialogo per violoncello e pianoforte (1932)
Tre canti per voce e pianoforte (1932)

Of the works listed above, I call out those that reflect more vividly some of the aesthetic thoughts Scelsi wrote while in Lausanne. They are:

1. *Quattro poemi* (Four Poems) for piano (1934–1937) represents the beginning of a stream of consciousness deriving from Scelsi's immersion in the music of Scriabin and Alban Berg that fascinated the composer throughout the 1940s.

The first poem, "Une derniére fois la terre," dedicated to Dorothy Kate Ramsden, was premiered in Rome at *Palazzo Doria Pamphili* on 9 November 1937 by pianist Ornella Puliti Santoliquido in a concert organized by *Gli amici della musica da camera*. On 11 June 1942, pianist Nikita Magaloff offered another performance of "Une derniére fois la terre" in Lausanne at the *Istituto Italiano di Cultura* as noted in the prologue. On that occasion the title of the piece was changed from the original French to the Italian "La terra un'ultima volta." The second poem, "Comme un cri traverse un cerveau," is indeed a psychological entanglement of motives, gestures, and arpeggios leading to the great serenity permeating the next poem, "Chemin du rêve," a beautiful "song without words" wrought in a surreal atmosphere. The fourth poem, "Passage du poète," *alla memoria di Alban Berg*, is the most extended and complex piece of the set. Quotations from Berg's *Piano Sonata* op. 1 (1909) are sprinkled liberally throughout the poem, making it Scelsi's declaration of admiration for the great composer who died on 24 December 1935.[3]

2. *12 Preludi (prima serie)*. Scelsi composed a total of forty-eight piano preludes and a forty-ninth for piano four-hands organized in four series.[4] The poetics of the first group of twelve short pieces alternate between the reality of the piano's idiomatic technique and contemplative visions. (1) *Martellato (senza pedale)* opens the series with a mechanical hammering on the keyboard followed by (2) a very sustained dirge dedicated to the memory of English poet T. G. Winans. (3) *Agitato molto liberamente ma sostenuto* dusts off the keyboard with a swarm of triplets, at times interrupted—like hiccups—by duplets and short holds. (4) *Moderato (etereo ed evanescente)* is a most delicate web of arabesques dedicated to Piero Coppola (1888–1971), in Italian composer-conductor active in the 1930s in Paris and later in Lausanne at the time of Scelsi's extensive sojourns in both cities. (5) This prelude is formed

by parables of ascending and descending gestures. It is dedicated to Raffaele d'Alessandro (1911–1959), a Swiss composer/organist who studied with Nadia Boulanger. His music reflected an anti-Romantic stance appealing to many young composers. He settled in Lausanne in 1940. (6) *Agitato* is like a battery of sextuplets restrained by triple-forte triplets. It is also dedicated to a Swiss musician, the Bernese pianist Magdi Rufer. (7) *Molto cantato* is a triple-soft study in chordal suppleness in which the melodies seem to emanate from the chords' reverberation. (8) *Delicato*. Similarly, to Prelude no. 5, this piece showcases six ascending rapid gestures followed by four descending ones. (9) *Agitato sostenuto* is a rhythmically asymmetric legato study dedicated to celebrated French pianist Alfred Cortot. (10) *Scorrevole, con poco pedale* is a brush-through-the keyboard by quadruplets of sixteenth notes played by alternating right and left hands. (11) *Drammatico, senza pedali, come timpani* is perhaps the most enticing of the twelve preludes. Stravinskian in its dry, percussion-like chords and abrupt rhythms, the piece is dedicated to celebrated Russian (later Swiss) pianist Nikita Magaloff. (12) *Allucinato* foreshadows, through its alarmingly disorienting sense of hallucination, the intuition of sound depth whose pursuit characterized Scelsi's late compositions.

3. *Variazioni e Fuga* is dedicated to the memory of Anton von Webern who died in 1945. It is Scelsi's most overt homage to pointillism imbued with dodecaphonic hints. Although some critics have asserted that Scelsi was the first Italian composer to adopt the twelve-tone system ahead of Luigi Dallapiccola, Scelsi never fully subscribed to the Schoenbergian system, preferring instead to adopt a sui generis serialism like many other composers of the 1930s and 1940s.

Variazioni e Fuga consists of sixteen contrasting aphoristic pieces preceding an elaborate Fugue (*Andante sostenuto, forte e deciso martellato senza pedale*) which leads the pianist through a tour-de-force of notable strength and virtuosity. Although academically dry, this piece reveals moments of authentic pathos and the sense of cantabile which distinguishes Scelsi's music from that of his Schoenberg-oriented contemporaries.

4. *Sonata* for piano is a grand pianistic exploit resembling the architecture of a baroque cathedral seen through the eyes of a late Romantic piano virtuoso. The first movement, *Sinfonia*, opens with a ponderous dotted rhythm played in octaves that one would expect to develop into a severe contrapuntal structure. Instead, Scelsi crumbles his material into a labyrinth in which ornamental thematic variations give way to episodes of virtuosity. These episodes alternate with cantabile urged on by a tight counterpoint that

overshadows the articulation of many a fine point. The second movement, *Largo*, is a passacaglia that, in contrast to the preceding classical Sinfonia, evokes magnificent piano sonorities one might find in the best moments of Franz Liszt's *Sonata in B Minor*. It is interesting to note that Scelsi's *Largo* was performed by Nikita Magaloff, a Liszt specialist, as a stand-alone piece in the program of the Lausanne 1942 concert discussed in the prologue. The Sonata's third movement, *Fuga*, is built on a rapid staccato subject and a lyrical counter subject that quickly threads a contrapuntal web of episodes of singular complexity. The *Coda*, marked *Più sostenuto*, brings the work to conclusion in a full, resonant fashion.

5. The *Trio per violino, violoncello e pianoforte* (1939) discussed in the prologue.

6. *Quartetto per due violini, viola e violoncello* is unquestionably the gem of the "De Santis Catalogue." Published in miniature score format bearing the now famous striking photo portrait of the composer, the *Quartetto* became the "calling card" that Scelsi sent to interested groups, festivals promoters, radio station programmers, and admirers. He thought highly of this work that premiered in Rome at Palazzo Sermoneta on 16 June 1948 by the Quartetto di Radio Roma (Vittorio Emanuele, Dandolo Sentuti, violini; Emilio Berengo Gardin, viola; Bruno Morselli, cello) and in Paris on 11 June 1949 by *Le Quatuor de Paris* (Georges Tessier, Maurice Hugon, violins, Jaques Baldut, viola, Roger Albin, cello) whose recorded tape Scelsi "played" in his home for musicians curious about his music and for those he wished to be interested in performing his music.[5] So, the *Quartetto* became for many the point of initiation to the Scelsi world we discuss in the last section of this book. For now, suffice it to say that this work, composed at the peak of Scelsi's so-called expressive atonality phase, held then and continues to hold a place in the string quartet literature of the post-1945 era.

Giacinto Scelsi and his mother were determined to bring to the stage the composer's *opus magnum*, the Cantata for chorus and Orchestra titled *La nascita del Verbo* (1944–48). The work, lasting some thirty-two minutes, was as complex and ambitious as a late Scriabin visionary fresco like *Prometheus: The Poem of Fire*, Op. 60 (1910), great in terms of expectations but tame in the result.

Luciano Martinis offered a vivid reconstruction of the preparatory phase of *La nascita del Verbo* by stitching together every scrap of paper he could find regarding the chaotic assemblage of sketches, scoring, extractions of instrumental and vocal parts, preparation of a piano reduction for possible publication, and so on.[6] A team of professionals, including copyists Giorgio Cangemi and Mario Lattanzi, and composers like Vieri Tosatti and Mario Zafred, worked frenetically under donna Giovanna's hawkish eye and purse to prepare the performing score and parts for the work's world premiere on Monday 28 November 1949 at the Théâtre des Champs-Elysées in Paris with the French National Orchestra conducted by Roger Désormiere and the French Radio Chorus directed by Yvonne Gouverné. The work was well received and heard by thousands as the concert was broadcast live by the French National Radio. A recording tape of the performance ended up in Scelsi's hands and was later transferred to disc.[7]

La nascita del Verbo ("La Naissance du Verbe") was performed again on 28 June 1950 at the Grand Auditorium de l'Institute Belge de Radiodiffusion by the Grande Orchestre Symphonique conducted by Franz André and the choir directed by René Mazy and Jan Van Bouwel. It was not performed again until 2005 at the *Festival "Wien Modern."*[8]

La nascita del Verbo represents a milestone in Scelsi's long and troublesome journey to appreciation and fame. It served to conclude a period of the composer's life as a wandering creative spirit in search of directions. Although *La nascita del Verbo* may complement Scelsi's aesthetic writings of the Lausanne period, one must keep in mind that while words can be spoken, read, and debated, music requires a different, much more complex type of acceptance and historical placement within a determined milieu. Therefore, we cannot think of *La nascita del Verbo* and its eventual historical position in the European and especially Italian music of the time without having to compare it to the works of his contemporaries like Olivier Messiaen's *Turangalîla Symphonie*, premiered in Boston on 2 December 1949 by Leonard Bernstein, and at the Aix-en-Provence Festival by Roger Dèsormiere on 25 July 1950 or Goffredo Petrassi's *Salmo IX* (1934), *Magnificat* (1938–1941), *Coro di morti* (1941), *Noche Oscura* (1950), Luigi Dallapiccola's *Canti di Prigionia* (1938–1941), and Casella's *Missa solemnis "pro pace"* (1944). These were some of the orchestral-choral masterpieces that defined a time in the history of Western music, everything else was of lesser significance.

Giacinto Scelsi, a very intelligent man, became aware of this situation, and experienced a crisis of existential proportion that required him to totally regain his physical and mental health. He sought relief and spiritual renewal in Eastern philosophical thoughts. His efforts guided him toward a reinvention of the Self, the Mount Everest he successfully scaled!

Post Scriptum

Decades later, French journalist and writer Jacques Drillon asked Scelsi about his sojourn in Switzerland during the war, to which Scelsi replied: "Switzerland is an extraordinary country. One only thinks of snow, skiing, doctors, and clinics. Yes, it is true, of course, but there are more drunks in Switzerland than in France, more divorces than in England, more murders, more suicides than anywhere else, more debauchery than in Paris; but it is all kept underground. I was there in a psychiatric clinic with the crazy people. I played billiards with them; I gave lectures that did not go well. I am still unwell. All creators are crazy. What about my madness? I will not discuss it. But the dark side of the moon does exist."[9]

Notes

1. Katie Boyle, *What This Katie Did: An Autobiography* (London: Weidenfeld and Nicolson, 1980), 96.

2. The De Santis-Scelsi publishing agreement was ultimately rescinded because of the Scelsi family's dissatisfaction with the publisher's disregard for their agreed-upon release time schedule and distribution effectiveness of the composer's works.

3. In 1937, Scelsi prepared an orchestral version of this piece under the title *Poème dédié à la mémoire d'Alban Berg / Poema (ad Alban Berg) / Passage du poète*. It has remained unpublished and unrecorded.

4. See the world premiere recording of Scelsi's complete *Preludi per pianoforte* by pianist Alessandra Ammara (Arts Music – GEMA 47721-8 (2009).

5. For the genesis of *Le Quatuor de Paris* recording see Martinis. "La prima edizione discografica di Giacinto Scelsi: il 'Quatuor à cordes:' Cronaca di una ricerca in *i suoni, le onde* . . . n. 27, 2, 2011: 3–9.

6. Luciano Martinis, "La Nascita del Verbo. Una cantata per coro e orchestra di Giacinto Scelsi" in *I suoni, le onde* . . . n. 12, 1, 2004: 3–13.

7. Luciano Martinis, "La Naissance du Verbe: Una ricerca conclusa" in *I suoni, le onde* . . . n. 30, 1, 2013: 9–10.

8. Festival "Wien Modern." Konzerthaus Vienna, 25 November 2005. Vienna Radio Symphony Orchestra conducted by Peter Rundel, and Concentus Vocalis, Wiener Kammerchor, directed by Johannes Kalitzke. The work, published by Editions Salabert was recorded live and issued by Mode Records, New York as Volume 6 of Mode's Giacinto Scelsi Edition in 2006.

9. Quoted by Jacques Drillon in "Les casquettes de Scelsi" in *Le Nouvel Observateur*, 3–9 avril 1987. See Kanach 2006, fn. 2, 14.

PART II

CHAPTER EIGHT

∼

Introduction

> "*Aspire to everything*
> *want nothing*"
>
> —Giacinto Scelsi[1]

Rome 1952–1954

From the arabesques of *Tetratkys* (1959) and the architectural embroideries of *Xnoybis* (1964) to the gravity of *Aiôn* (1961), sound in the music of Giacinto Scelsi is in a state of constant motion, evolution, and continuous becoming. The conceptual form of sound depth is spiral-like following helical trajectories—which, despite being sinuously irregular and imperfect, reach the exact center of a perfect sphere.

So, the sonic tridimensionality envisioned by Scelsi does not follow the rigorous rules of perspective. In fact, it bears no numerical, proportional, symmetric, or geometric calculations. The function of music is to express "a part, and maybe the greater part of images produced in the consciousness by the creative forces," wrote Scelsi about the four elements of mankind. Those elements are rhythm, emotion, intellect, and psyche juxtaposed to music creation and its manifestations.[2] In his subsequent essays, *The Evolution of Harmony*, and *The Evolution of Rhythm*, Scelsi's perspective shifted toward a more historical approach by considering the music and the writings of Wagner, Debussy, Strauss, Berg, Scriabin, Stravinsky, Honegger, Mossolov, and some indigenous music from around the world.

Notwithstanding such a diverse chronological approach, the focus of Scelsi's interest remained the same: the understanding of the balance occurring between the fundamental stages of mankind. He wrote: "Our study is concerned solely with the evolution of harmony in the context of the balance of the fundamental elements in European art and society."[3]

Such a historical perspective emphasizes the rhythmic dimension while forging contacts with the universal dynamism. Regarding Stravinsky's *The Rite of Spring*, Scelsi opined that affectivity and intellect lost their hold on human beings as they dove into the primordial cosmic pulse, a primal movement akin perhaps to the rhythmic breathing of Prometheus unchained, the archetypical figure who freed himself from his chains and appeared naked, terrifying, and immense before the world.[4]

Scelsi was also an unchained Prometheus in search of a "fire," the primal energy of the sound he wished to capture in a cosmic dimension to transform it into a physical and perceptible sound without provoking the ire of the gods. On the contrary, Scelsi's encounter with the Devic dimension determined his relationship with the sound and formed the foundations of his creative process.

The development of Scelsi's theoretical thinking occurred mostly during his "golden" exile at the *Hôtel de la Paix* in Lausanne discussed in part I of this book as a place of many encounters, friendships, and high society. Scelsi's autobiography *Il sogno 101* is a treasure chest of detailed episodes about this segment of his biographical journey. He observed that "Besides being the refuge of thinkers, writers—and not only the refuge but the congenial choice for many of them—Switzerland is also teeming with spiritualistic, religious, and esoteric centers. [. . .] These centers promote a great many activities, followers, and proselytes who in the summer adjourn to the lakes or mountains for meditation courses, spiritual and even physical exercises in addition to the yoga schools which are quite numerous. So, all this [. . .] creates a concentration of various elements that are difficult to find in other countries."[5]

It is in such a milieu that the roots of Scelsi's "musical system" stood firm. The presence of Rudolf Steiner in Dornach where he had his first Goetheanum built fully in wood, constitutes a solid center of gravity from which the theosophic and anthroposophical thought radiated in increasingly extended concentric waves. Scelsi remained involved with such thinking throughout his life as confirmed by Steiner's volumes, *L'essenza della musica e l'esperienza del suono nell'uomo*, and *L'initiation: ou Comment acquérir des connaissances sur le mondes superieurs*, kept in his personal library.[6]

Echoes or even the direct attendance to the annual colloquia taking place at Casa Eranos in Ascona near Monte Verità organized by Olga Froebe-Kapteyn, influenced Scelsi through innumerable suggestions. Those colloquia were considered as "the official gathering of medical doctors, scientists, psychologists, and psychoanalysts joined by specialists and personalities hailing from all over the world [. . .] the finest thinkers and artists."[7] However, no traces of the *Eranos-Jahrbuch* published since 1933 were found in Scelsi's library, just notebooks filled with fragmentary commentaries jotted down after lectures delivered by Steiner and others.

Sound and Music and *Art and Knowledge*, the two essays comprising part II of the present book, were conceived in dialogical form as ample reflections upon questions posed to unknown, perhaps nonexistent interlocutors. They were meant to create a unified text that adopted the author's new *modus scribendi* which become his norm of communication through the early 1970s when he dictated his autobiography *Il sogno 101* into a tape recorder. Thereafter, these recorded "conversations" were transcribed as monologues spoken in first person and addressed to three imaginary individuals Scelsi referred to as the "chatterers."

The two texts in question were "dictated" and then "transcribed" in the early 1950s. They correspond to a creative phase that employed musical instruments capable of producing what can be defined as "moldable intonation."[8] The piano, on the other hand, Scelsi's favorite instrument since infancy, was set aside gradually as a secondary presence.

Scelsi's Swiss years, a period of aphasia, silence, reflection, listening, and stimuli ignited an intellectual as well as spiritual crisis. Discussions arose about the black and white keys of the piano, the conception of heights, intervals, and the relationships between the notes still anchored to the centuries-old tempered system.

The rupture of the diaphragm separating note from sound, and the practice of "de-composing and re-composing, implied a fully changed point of view from the honored Western musical tradition based above all on systemic combining and overlapping. Thus, the new perspective involved not composing (juxtaposing, overlapping), but de-composing, or to put it more simply, *running* the sound."[9] Running the sound means in essence running a revolution as "the real revolutionaries are those who have modified our relationship with the sound." [10]

In *Sound and Music*, the aesthetical thought reaches out toward mature completeness. Harmonics, vibrations, frequencies, perceptible sound, spheric sound, psychic sound, all become necessary to restore to the sound its inherent quintessential vibration.

Scelsi's return to Italy from Switzerland represents more than a geographic, logistical move. Once back in Rome, Scelsi's biographical uncertainties started to unravel as he searched for and found new inspirations, relationships, horizons, experimentations. Much can be said about Rome in the 1950s, a city of contradictions: cultured and subversive, provincial and cosmopolitan, rational and mystic, intellectual, refined and easygoing. However, what emerged from Scelsi's transition was the *Weltanschauung* that from being partial and uncertain, revealed itself to the fullest: In 1957, the novel Prometheus treaded his metaphorical chains for the electric cables of the ondiola.[11]

A small, portable proto electronic instrument related to the French *clavioline* invented by Constant Martin in 1947, the ondiola's mechanism includes a monophonic three to six octave range keyboard, oscillator, condensers, and filters capable of acting on a chosen fundamental sound by modifying its timbre. A series of switches placed at the front of the keyboard allows the operator (player) to modulate the length of sound wave, produce glissandos, obtain micro intervals, and shape the vibrato by controlling almost endlessly the emission of the electronically generated sound.

Scelsi's maneuvering of the ondiola's sonic resources concerned the more or less periodical and rapid temporal fluctuations of one or more sound parameters (timbre, amplitude, and height), and new techniques he experimented with for a unique scope: to "compose" the sound vibrations in order to access a sonic third dimension.

The intuition of sound depth was at the core of Scelsi's new musical endeavor which materialized immediately as the sound, once set in motion, becomes, indeed, his "ultimate" sound.

There are no scientific or technological devices to be found in Scelsi's workshop—just two ondiolas and two tape recorders. The sound was shaped through long improvisations which was then "captured," recorded, and stored by a support mechanism capable of preserving it at the time of happening. "Sound exists on its own without the music. . . . Music evolves in time. Sound is atemporal. Sound is power," Scelsi reminded us.[12]

Art and Knowledge, Scelsi's last aesthetical writing, distilled the essence of his sonic logos. He wrote: "Let us say: creative artistic faculty. What is it? It is the ability to arrest motion, to crystallize an instant of duration, to tear it from oneself—and to project this instant through an effort of the entire being, in a verbal, sonic or plastic matter."[13]

When considering the historical and geographical position of the artist in society, Scelsi's human and artisanal conflict is never avoided, forgotten, or neglected. Indeed, Scelsi pays homage to the technical work and to the artist's ability without hiding his detachment from such aspects.[14]

The conception of the creative act has finally found its set of codifications: arresting, crystallizing, freeing (or detaching, perhaps), projecting. A full assertion, therefore, of what was proposed *in nuce* in the writings of 1942.[15] He irreversibly crossed the threshold, thus theoretic reflections, creative conceptions, and musical practice converged and blended into a unified thought.

Scelsi's peculiar stylistic code finds its manifestation in the works for solo instruments or small ensembles (string and winds particularly) but also, and above all, in the great choral orchestral frescos of the early 1960s which defined the idiomatic style that sealed Scelsi's stature as one of the most radical and innovative artists of the twentieth century.

Notes

1. See Octologo, 105
2. See The Meaning of Music, 16
3. See The Evolution of Harmony, 27
4. See The Evolution of Rhythm, 35 "It is the rhythmic breathing of 'Prometheus in chains,' a primordial struggle, a dynamic urgency—he, the true giant breaking his last chains appeared among humans, naked, terrifying, and immense."
5. See *Il sogno 101*, a cura di Luciano Martinis e Alessandra Carlotta Pellegrini, Macerata: Quodlibet, 2010, 50.
6. Rudolf Steiner, *L'essenza della musica e l'esperienza del suono nell'uomo*, tradotta da Dante Vigevani, Milano, Editrice Antroposofica, 1973, and *L'initiation: ou Comment acquérir des connaissances sur les modes supérieurs*, tradotto da Maria Steiner, Paris: La science spirituelle, 1948.
7. Quoted from a lecture delivered by Rudolf Steiner and translated into Italian by Baronessa Grünwald. A bound typescript of it was kept by Scelsi among his personal papers.
8. As an example, here are the titles of some works reflecting the above statement: Suite per flauto e clarinetto (1953), *Divertimento no. 2* per violino solo (1954), *Pwyll* per flauto solo (1954), *Quays* per flauto contralto o flauto in do (1954), *Tre studi* per clarinetto in mi bemolle (1954), *Preghiera per un'ombra* per clarinetto in si bemolle (1954), *Divertimento n. 3* per violino solo (1955), *Divertimento n. 4* per violino solo (1955), *Coelocanth* per viola sola (1955), *Hyxos* per flauto in sol, gong e campanella (1955).

9. Tristan Murail, "Scelsi de-compositore," in *Giacinto Scelsi, Viaggio al centro del suono*, a cura di Pierre Albert Castanet e Nicola Cisternino, La Spezia, Luna Editore, 2001, 83.

10. Ibid., 84

11. 1957 is the date written on a payment receipt that F. X. Féron attributes to acquisition of Scelsi's second ondiola not the first. Of the various writings on the ondiola subject, see Elisabetta Piras, "Improvvisazioni di Giacinto Scelsi: il caso problematico dell'ondiola," *in i suoni, le onde . . .* , n. 19–20, Roma, Fondazione Isabella Scelsi, 2008, pp. 3–9; François-Xavier Féron, "Les variations dans la vibration: vibrato, tremolos et trilles dans la Trilogie —*Les trois stades de l'homme* (1956–1965) pour violoncelle seul de Giacinto Scelsi," in "Scelsi incombustible," *Filigrane*, n. 15, Maggio 2012 (monographic issue a cura di Makis Solomos e Alessandra Carlotta Pellegrini), https://revues.mshparisnord.fr/filigrane/index.php?id=516 (accessed 5 June 2022).

12. See Giacinto Scelsi, *Il sogno 101*, 6.

13. See *Art and Knowledge*, 90

14. Ibid., 92 "Yes, of course: It is difficult to isolate the artist from his milieu. We know too well what the artist's place is in a corner of the world, at a point in history—especially in the history that we understand, which is the city where he learned his craft, who his teachers or his contemporaries were—the artist cannot be isolated from all that."

15. See *The Meaning of Music*, 20. "In conclusion, let it be said that all art is nothing but projection onto matter, be it verbal, sound or plastic, of images created by the fundamental elements. Through the analysis of these elements in a work of art, we discover that the artist's creative impulses are externalized and crystallized."

CHAPTER NINE

Sound and Music

So, do you want to talk about music? Fine but first: What do you mean by sound and what do you mean by music? Music cannot exist without sound, yet sound exists very well without music. So, it seems that sound is more important. Let us start with this point. As you know, there is physical sound, which is produced by one vibration or frequency in the air. Vibrations or frequencies provoke different types of sound waves. It would take me several days to describe them phenomenologically.

As you know, the fundamental sound generates harmonics — the octave, the fifth, the third, and so on. If the sound is complex, then the quantity of harmonics is enormous.

You may not have the idea of a pure sinusoidal sound devoid of harmonics, nor the complexity required to obtain it scientifically.

Yes, the spectrum of sounds perceivable by our ears is limited while a reality is infinitely larger. In general, animals hear more sounds similarly, of course, to the mechanical devices made for such a purpose. These devices even manage to perceive and calculate the vibrations emitted by certain beams invisible to our eyes, and to calculate the curves of oscillations occurring within the sound, and so on. But all that would take our discussion too far afield.

In addition, sound is spherical, but by listening to it we may think it possesses only two dimensions: pitch and duration —a third dimension, depth, in some way escapes us although we know of its existence. The higher and lower harmonics (heard less frequently) sometimes give us the impression of

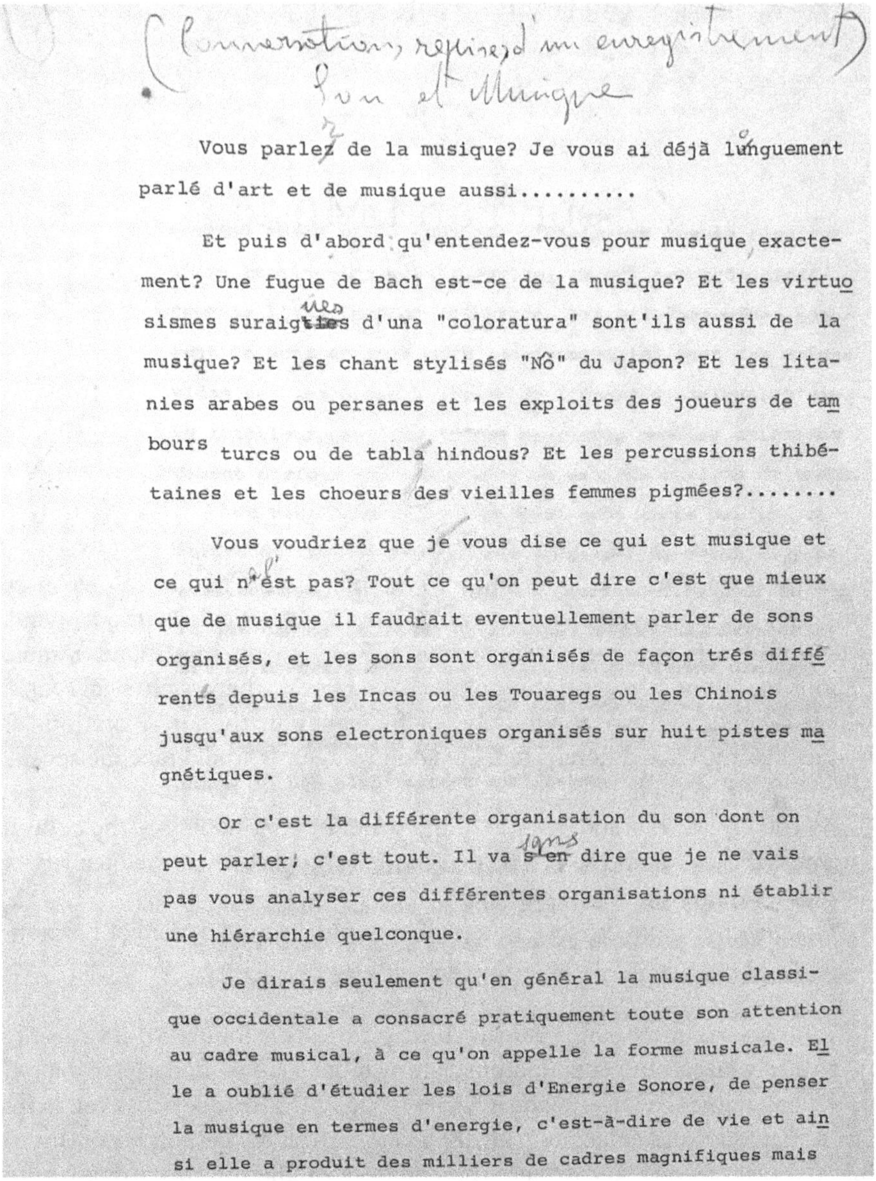

(Conversation, reprises d'un enregistrement)
Son et Musique

Vous parlez de la musique? Je vous ai déjà longuement parlé d'art et de musique aussi..........

Et puis d'abord qu'entendez-vous pour musique, exactement? Une fugue de Bach est-ce de la musique? Et les virtuosismes suraigües d'una "coloratura" sont'ils aussi de la musique? Et les chant stylisés "Nô" du Japon? Et les litanies arabes ou persanes et les exploits des joueurs de tambours turcs ou de tabla hindous? Et les percussions thibétaines et les choeurs des vieilles femmes pigmées?........

Vous voudriez que je vous dise ce qui est musique et ce qui n'est pas? Tout ce qu'on peut dire c'est que mieux que de musique il faudrait éventuellement parler de sons organisés, et les sons sont organisés de façon trés différents depuis les Incas ou les Touaregs ou les Chinois jusqu'aux sons electroniques organisés sur huit pistes magnétiques.

Or c'est la différente organisation du son dont on peut parler; c'est tout. Il va sans dire que je ne vais pas vous analyser ces différentes organisations ni établir une hiérarchie quelconque.

Je dirais seulement qu'en général la musique classique occidentale a consacré pratiquement toute son attention au cadre musical, à ce qu'on appelle la forme musicale. Elle a oublié d'étudier les lois d'Energie Sonore, de penser la musique en termes d'energie, c'est-à-dire de vie et ainsi elle a produit des milliers de cadres magnifiques mais

Figure 9.1a. *Son et Musique.* Typescript of working draft with initial autographed emendations by Giacinto Scelsi.
© Fondazione Isabella Scelsi. Roma

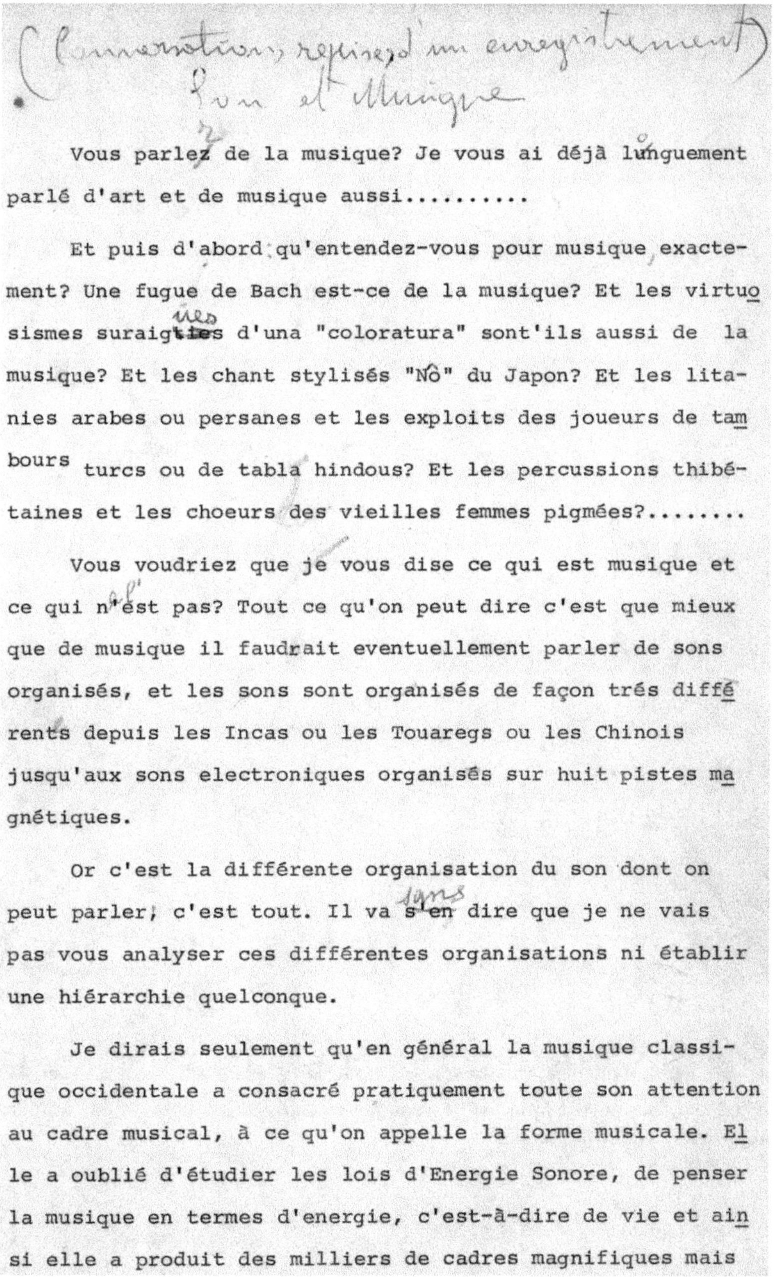

(Conversation, reprise d'un enregistrement)
Son et Musique

Vous parlez de la musique? Je vous ai déjà lo'nguement parlé d'art et de musique aussi..........

Et puis d'abord qu'entendez-vous pour musique exactement? Une fugue de Bach est-ce de la musique? Et les virtuosismes suraigües d'una "coloratura" sont'ils aussi de la musique? Et les chants stylisés "Nô" du Japon? Et les litanies arabes ou persanes et les exploits des joueurs de tambours turcs ou de tabla hindous? Et les percussions thibétaines et les choeurs des vieilles femmes pigmées?........

Vous voudriez que je vous dise ce qui est musique et ce qui n'est pas? Tout ce qu'on peut dire c'est que mieux que de musique il faudrait eventuellement parler de sons organisés, et les sons sont organisés de façon très différents depuis les Incas ou les Touaregs ou les Chinois jusqu'aux sons electroniques organisés sur huit pistes magnétiques.

Or c'est la différente organisation du son dont on peut parler; c'est tout. Il va sans dire que je ne vais pas vous analyser ces différentes organisations ni établir une hiérarchie quelconque.

Je dirais seulement qu'en général la musique classique occidentale a consacré pratiquement toute son attention au cadre musical, à ce qu'on appelle la forme musicale. Elle a oublié d'étudier les lois d'Energie Sonore, de penser la musique en termes d'energie, c'est-à-dire de vie et ainsi elle a produit des milliers de cadres magnifiques mais

Figure 9.1b. *Son et Musique.* Typescript of working draft with initial autographed emendations by Giacinto Scelsi.
© Fondazione Isabella Scelsi. Roma

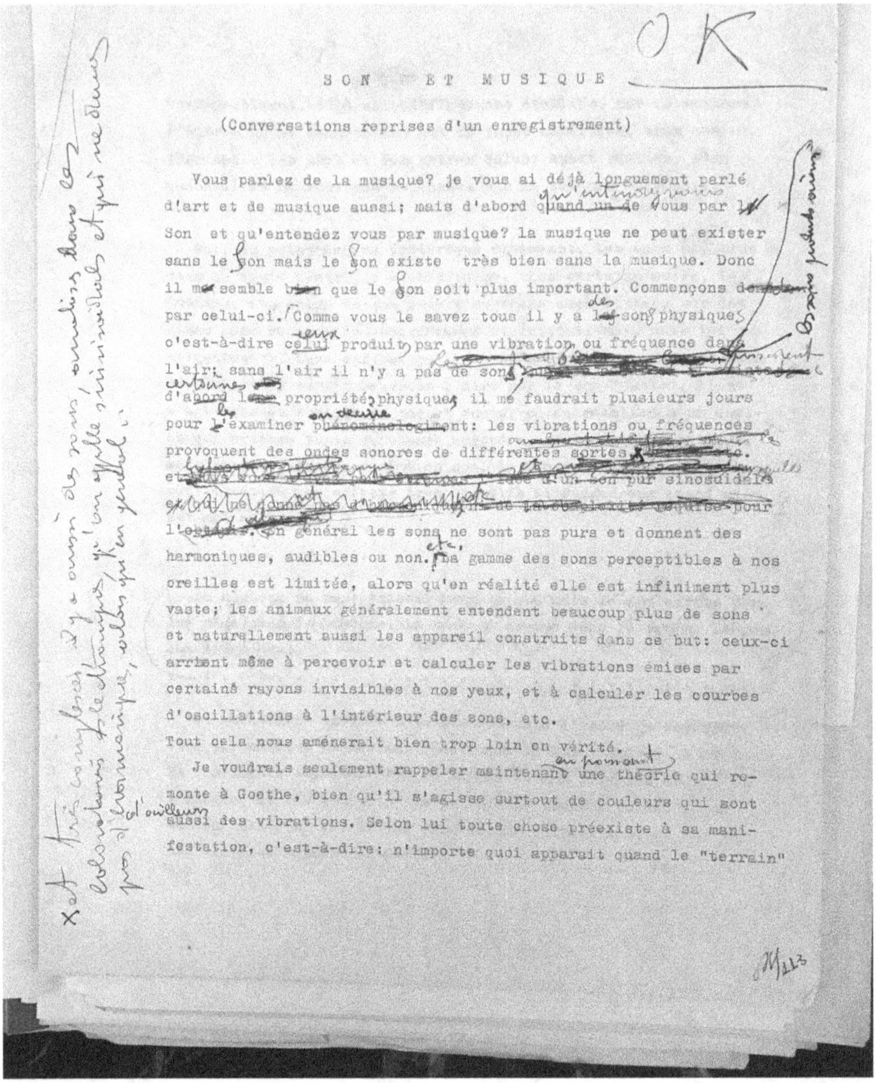

SON ET MUSIQUE

(Conversations reprises d'un enregistrement)

Vous parlez de la musique? je vous ai déjà longuement parlé d'art et de musique aussi; mais d'abord qu'entendez vous par le Son et qu'entendez vous par musique? la musique ne peut exister sans le Son mais le Son existe très bien sans la musique. Donc il me semble bien que le Son soit plus important. Commençons donc par celui-ci. Comme vous le savez tous il y a des sons physiques c'est-à-dire celui produit par une vibration ou fréquence dans l'air; sans l'air il n'y a pas de son.
d'abord les propriétés physiques il me faudrait plusieurs jours pour l'examiner phénoménologiquement: les vibrations ou fréquences provoquent des ondes sonores de différentes sortes
et ~~~~~~~~~~~~~~~~~~~~~~~~~~
~~~~~~
l'oreille. En général les sons ne sont pas purs et donnent des harmoniques, audibles ou non. La gamme des sons perceptibles à nos oreilles est limitée, alors qu'en réalité elle est infiniment plus vaste; les animaux généralement entendent beaucoup plus de sons et naturellement aussi les appareils construits dans ce but: ceux-ci arrivent même à percevoir et calculer les vibrations émises par certains rayons invisibles à nos yeux, et à calculer les courbes d'oscillations à l'intérieur des sons, etc.
Tout cela nous amènerait bien trop loin en vérité.

Je voudrais seulement rappeler maintenant une théorie qui remonte à Goethe, bien qu'il s'agisse surtout de couleurs qui sont aussi des vibrations. Selon lui toute chose préexiste à sa manifestation, c'est-à-dire; n'importe quoi apparaît quand le "terrain"

Figure 9.2a. *Son et Musique.* **Typescript of working draft with initial autographed emendations by Giacinto Scelsi.**
© Fondazione Isabella Scelsi. Roma

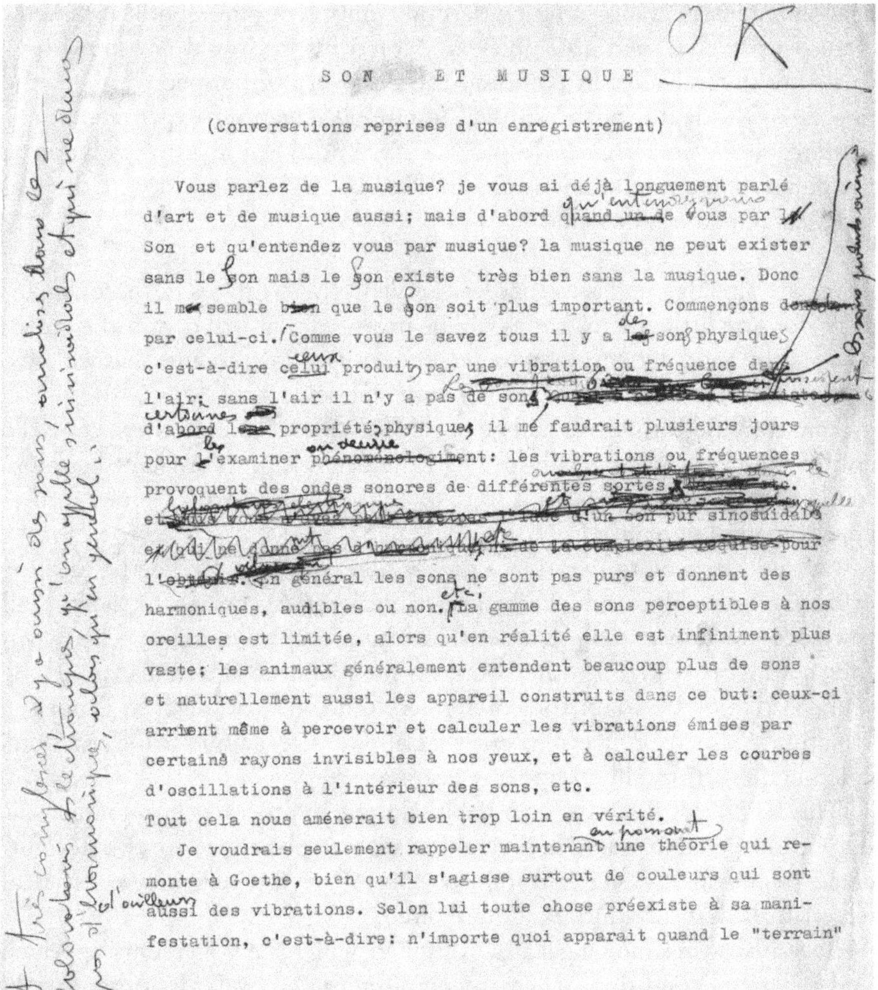

SON ET MUSIQUE

(Conversations reprises d'un enregistrement)

Vous parlez de la musique? je vous ai déjà longuement parlé d'art et de musique aussi; mais d'abord qu'entendez vous par le Son et qu'entendez vous par musique? la musique ne peut exister sans le Son mais le Son existe très bien sans la musique. Donc il me semble bien que le Son soit plus important. Commençons donc par celui-ci. Comme vous le savez tous il y a les sons physiques c'est-à-dire ceux produits par une vibration ou fréquence de l'air; sans l'air il n'y a pas de son. d'abord les propriétés physiques il me faudrait plusieurs jours pour l'examiner phénoménologiquement: les vibrations ou fréquences provoquent des ondes sonores de différentes sortes. et
l'objet. En général les sons ne sont pas purs et donnent des harmoniques, audibles ou non. La gamme des sons perceptibles à nos oreilles est limitée, alors qu'en réalité elle est infiniment plus vaste; les animaux généralement entendent beaucoup plus de sons et naturellement aussi les appareil construits dans ce but: ceux-ci arrivent même à percevoir et calculer les vibrations émises par certains rayons invisibles à nos yeux, et à calculer les courbes d'oscillations à l'intérieur des sons, etc.
Tout cela nous amènerait bien trop loin en vérité.
Je voudrais seulement rappeler maintenant une théorie qui remonte à Goethe, bien qu'il s'agisse surtout de couleurs qui sont aussi des vibrations. Selon lui toute chose préexiste à sa manifestation, c'est-à-dire: n'importe quoi apparait quand le "terrain"

Figure 9.2b. *Son et Musique*. Typescript of working draft with initial autographed emendations by Giacinto Scelsi.
© Fondazione Isabella Scelsi. Roma

a larger and more complex sound beyond duration or pitch, but it is difficult for us to perceive such a complexity. Moreover, we would not know how to notate it musically. In painting, the discovery of perspective gives the impression of depth, but in music, despite all advanced experimentations in stereophony and what have you, we have not been able to evolve from the duration and pitch dimensions and to receive the impression of the real spherical dimension of sound.

There are already eyeglasses that let you view photo images in three dimensions; for sure little microphones will be invented that will permit the receptivity of the third dimension of sound, or even new instruments that will give that same result without the need of auricular devices.

I am convinced that this will be possible in one way or another before the end of the century, especially through the acquisition of a faculty of more subtle perception or through a state of consciousness which allows a finer approximation of reality.

I would like now to mention a theory that goes back to Goethe, dealing primarily with colors, which are also vibrations. According to Goethe all things preexist their manifestations, meaning that anything appears when the "terrain" is ready. In other words: a number x of vibrations causes the sound "C" to be heard, or the color green to be seen; however, it is not the vibration x which produces it, but that allows it to manifest; for any note, color, and even any illness and any event.

This is a theory that alters our habitual thought processes in a unique way, but it can be demonstrated in several instances, especially when the "terrain" element prevails, to say nothing—of course—of the religious or mystical experiences that substantiate it quite often.

Recently, some biological discoveries in which new elements appeared under certain conditions, seem to confirm this as well. In other words, everything exists in a latent state of energy. Everything would preexist in the cosmos in all possible forms, and their manifestations would occur—at every level—from matter to spirit when the "terrain" is favorable.

Human beings can increase and enlarge the range of the "terrain." Certainly, other sounds and other colors will respond and reveal themselves. Something to think about.

But let us return to the sound. There are other aspects of it. The psychic aspect of inner sounds: those that we hear in meditation, and those that exist at higher and transcendental levels. We will address them later.

Yes, we can consider sound as the cosmic force which is the basis of everything. There is a beautiful definition that says: "Sound is the first movement of stillness," and this is the beginning of Creation. Sound at rest (if one can say so) is spherical but, being in essence dynamic, it can assume any form and become multidimensional. While being cosmic in nature, it can be "activated" and "used" by, say, human beings. In a certain occult tradition, we find a very interesting idea, namely that the sound possesses three bodies: the physical body, the psychic body, and the logical body. This means that the end is creative at all levels.

Yes, in esoteric terms sounds are also used in Tibetan tantric magic, by certain black populations, by shamans, and, according to some occultists, on extra sensorial and supernatural levels as well. But be careful here! Most importantly, there must be no confusion about sounds. I have much to say about the "right" sound. This has nothing to do with the right "note," compared to any European, African, or Asian atonal, tonal system, but about the very essence of the sound. Sound is energy, and it can produce very negative and dangerous effects when misused.

In the Yoga of sound, the adepts manage—as I said before—to hear their personal sound and then the Devic sounds. Personal sound leads to the perception of the supernatural world, at the same time as it produces an inner balance, which is precisely at the core of this Yoga. Often the sound also manifests its color, but this is something else. All this naturally debunks the importance of the "right" sound, whether it emanates from the human voice or an instrument. Therefore, I think that monody can more easily render this accuracy than orchestral or symphonic works.

According to the Yoga of sound, ecstasy and enlightenment are the effect of the "right" sound. The vibrations create a form shaped according to the law of affinity, agreeing to its resonant chamber, but also transforming it.

This is the basis of the doctrine, because according to it, SOUND is the source of all revelation revealed from within. In the *Vedas* this sound is called *Anahad*, which means *limitless sound*.

I cannot tell you what the technique is to attain it. It is part of the "Laya and Kriya-Yoga" and includes special exercises of very calm breathing and the knowledge of the effect of sounds on our physical organs and subtle centers. There are Hindu and Tibetan texts that should be read; I will just recommend those of Patanjali, which are classics, but I assure you that a few simple daily exercises are supposedly more beneficial than a dozen books.

But let us return to the musical elements. Previously I spoke about how they conform to mankind: rhythm to vitality; melody to emotion; harmony to the psyche, structure to the intellect; and the effect of these elements on the human organism.

Yes, from that emerge the therapeutic attempts, for example. There are already books on sound therapy. Sound vibrations affect living cells. They are shown to affect the most spiritual element. I could make a long digression on therapeutic qualities, already scientifically established, because of many other qualities one can only speak empirically, although—for me—both are also rebellious, even when they are not recognized by official science.

But we must go back to music. Music evolves in time, sound is timeless. But what do we mean by music, exactly? A fugue by Bach, is it music? And the shrill virtuosities of a *coloratura* soprano, are they also music? And the stylized Nô songs of Japan? And the Arabic or Persian litanies, the exploits of Turkish drum players or the Hindu *tabla*? What about Tibetan percussion, and the choirs of the old Pygmy women?

Would you want me to tell you what is music and what is not? All one can probably say is that, rather than about music, one ought to speak eventually about organized sounds—and sounds have been organized in very different ways since the Incas, the Tuaregs, or the Chinese up to electronic sounds organized on eight magnetic tape tracks.

So, one could speak of different ways of organizing sound. That is all. It goes without saying that I am not going to analyze for you those various ways of organization or establish a hierarchy of some sort.

I will say only that, in general, Western classical music has devoted practically all its attention to the musical structure, the so-called musical form. It has neglected to study the laws of sound energy, to think of music in terms of energy, which is life. Thus, it has produced thousands of magnificent structures which are often empty or meaningless because they are nothing but the result of constructive imagination, which is very different than creative imagination. Melodies travel from sound to sound, but the intervals are hollow abysses because the notes lack sonic energy. The inner space is empty.

I will give you an example: we have very beautiful church bells everywhere in Europe—at least, there were many that have since been melted to make cannons or shells. Still, there are many left, ancient or modern, which are treated in the same manner, meaning mistreated by sacristans who pull ropes as best they can, without rhythm, mindlessly, and the heaviest ones are being operated by an electric motor.

In the East, in India, Japan, China, or Tibet, gongs—which play the same role in temples—are struck with utmost respect and in a very particular way down to the smallest little high-pitched bell, as each sound must produce its proper effect.

Yes, it is true that we have Stradivarius, Guarneri, and so on, marvelous people and unique artisans, but composers did not know how to exploit these superb instrumental crafts from their sound's point of view, using them to write and perform an enormous quantity of "pieces" for violin or cello.

I must add that the Europeans did indeed demand such "pieces" of music and the virtuosos were not really concerned whether the "pieces" they played were good or bad.

Moreover, despite my full admiration for Stradivarius, Guarneri, and the others, I suspect that they were mostly interested in the beauty and perfection of the sound from the acoustical point of view. For Westerners, harmonics are generally an acoustical factor; the Asians, on the other hand, find in harmonics a spiritual element that goes beyond the physical.

Yes, of course. For some time here in Europe, and even more so in America, sound and its own energy have been studied; in that sense, we have come closer to the Asian concept—say from Webern and Varèse to electronic music. We care less about structure, and we could argue that it has been destroyed, furiously even, by aleatoric techniques and more. Only, in most cases, it is still an intellectual, scientific, and mathematical or pure acoustical research.

The world may have been created with numbers not by numbers (said Goethe).

You ask me whether the music of Bach, Beethoven, or Mozart is empty. My answer is that among the enormous amounts of music they wrote, there are, indeed, a large number of empty works, and when they are not, it is because the composers received, in a certain state of consciousness, elements of perception of a higher order which have, in part if not in total, compensated for the organizational system of composition.

Also, I would tell you that Bach, Beethoven, Mozart, and some others do not constitute the whole [spectrum] of Western music. Except for the best, of the most consistently inspired (who also, moreover, could not always keep in touch with higher perceptions) the rest is indeed music quite empty of this sound energy which is in turn something other than the perfection of certain forms of sonatas or symphonies, and has nothing to do either with rhythmic violence, melodic effusion, or orchestral gigantism.

Do you want me to tell you that the music of Bach and Mozart could not have brought down the walls of Jericho? Yes, it is a bit like that. But let us understand one another well. I have often affirmed that structure—the form—is an expression of the intellect and melody an expression of emotion; each element is fundamental in mankind, and none of its manifestations is in itself inferior to the other.

Each civilization, and each epoch of it, finds its own "terrain" to cultivate and, for Europe since the Middle Ages, it was a spirit of strict logic that had to assert and manifest itself in art—entirely as well as in its parts. Thus, fugues, imitations, and intricated movements of contrapuntal voices were part of a *modus operandi* that was intended specifically for them. In the Romantic era it was expression, the depiction of human psychological feelings.

For my part, I cannot prevent myself from seeing, to confine myself to Europe, the history and development of music from an angle other than that of historical criticism.

Which then? I once said I was a finalist. I believe that in the history of civilizations everything can be examined and studied from a different angle, both in the evolution of the arts and in that of the individuals called upon to assume a role in this evolution and who, most often, play it without realizing the occult reason why, at some point in their life or the life of the world, they are led to this *modus operandi* and not another, to accomplish their works.

I have already spoken to you another time about the constant evolution of the fundamental elements in mankind, their alternation or predominance. Naturally, this evolution manifests itself more or less clearly and in a general way in works of art because they basically remain as sensitive testimonies of the past.

Yes. Obviously with the precursors, new perceptions came to the fore of their consciousness a few years, or a few decades earlier than with the others. It follows, in these precursors, variations in the relationships between the fundamental elements which, in turn, determine a different way of looking at things and a new *modus operandi*. It is indeed through these precursors that the evolution of the world of art continues through the influence of their thoughts and their works. Sooner or later, these generate in all of society a new *Weltanschauung* and, consequently, a new *modus operandi*.

Yes, for sure, there are a thousand theories on the evolution of mankind and human society—if you want, speaking of the ape to an Einstein, or of a native American tribe in the United States of America.

Regarding my speaking to you about classical or modern composers individually—about one or another—it presupposes an analysis whose principles I have indicated to you, but between us, it is no way a matter of historical studies or criticism, but about understanding, as far as possible, the meaning of things.

So, we cannot really speak about music: what music, what music is, and when it is music, but only about the organization of sounds.

Regarding the evolution of music in the world, I cannot, for my part, disregard the Devic activity. What can one say about this activity? Nobody can—or would have the right—to say anything at all. I can only assure you that most "inspirations" come from higher planes and from contact with the Devas. Their role is—in a few words—to introduce new kinds of vibrations into the world, through sound. Since sound operates through laws of correspondence with the human elements, and since, it has been proven, on the other hand, that the repetition of a formula produces a particular physical, moral, or spiritual result, hence, the simple theory of Coué consisting of the repetition of a sentence to improve health and, of course, all the doctrine of the Hindu *japa* which are based on such repetition and involves absolutely spiritual realizations. Music, by the repetition of one sound or a sonic formula, through its relationship with the human fundamental elements, tends to produce and reproduce certain modifications in the balance of relationships. Moreover, the words of the formulas or the *japa* can provoke, through the power of their words, a spirit of antagonism.

This is obviously the reason for the existence, always, of certain kinds of music, both in religious rites and secular celebrations, and their use as military and warlike stimuli.

Generally, it is believed that music and all the arts are the product of their time. In reality, for one part—the only part that can be considered art—the opposite is true. All changes and innovations in musical style have invariably been followed by innovations in morals and politics. Such is, moreover, the logical consequence of what I have explained to you.

The "Devic" action affects only the evolution of the world, not to the benefit or glory of any individual. The individual is then the chosen channel, so far as it can be inspired to transmit a new type of music. This channel being too inadequate for the total reception of a Devic message, it would be unable to support it entirely: on one hand, because it would be contrary to all the channel's acquired notions, and on the other hand, because it would almost totally lack the technical means to manifest these messages. Moreover, the individual's psychophysical organism would be dangerously shaken to the risk of destruction. It happens often that a genius dies young or suffers serious misfortunes. The Devas must, therefore, in the case of the evolution of music and for any other evolution, consider the frailty of the incarnations and advance gradually, choosing from time-to-time certain individuals who are particularly gifted or "ready." This choice focuses on individuals whose qualities and aspirations we have examined earlier.

Many of the artists who have experienced the Devic action, however, have failed to control their lower energetic vehicles (to use Yoga terminology). This explains why the Devic contact is intermittent and the artists' inspiration inconsistent and of sporadic quality. Their psychophysical organism is incapable of becoming completely the vehicle necessary for Devic manifestation. This explains the problem that often preoccupies people: why men and women of genius who show such extraordinary artistic qualities of thought, or otherwise, are not models of integrity and why they fall or live on an average plane, or worse.

As I explained in other conversations, the ignorance of spiritual matters, of the means of contact with higher realities, is so great even among the most admirable artists and cultivated individuals that they are unable to consider the importance of the contact that [their] nature offers them at times.

The work that the Devas do with artists is only the preparation, intellectually, emotionally, and psychically, for an evolution and the ultimate manifestation of a music that we cannot even conceive.

Yes, it is true that there is also music with a transcendental character which defies any analytical organization, as well as any human comprehension.

Some privileged beings have heard sounds, melodies, or harmonies that may be qualified as "out of this world," just like certain colors that belong to this same plane. There are very many accounts on the part of the saints and a whole literature and iconography which derive from them: musician angels with trumpets, lyres, or flutes; the accounts of Swedenborg or Jakob Boehme to the marvelous music heard by them and sometimes by whole crowds in various places. According to witness accounts, these melodies were of an inconceivable delicacy or a sonic luminosity impossible for humans to reach.

Innumerable are the cases of hearing supernatural choirs in chapels, around dying people, or around saints. We can also count by the thousands the individual experiences of people who heard music that was not of this world. Everyone agreed that it is impossible to describe the extraordinary power of these sonorities which were like an ocean of marvelous music that no orchestra could ever reproduce. More than a listening experience, it was a feeling of living the essence of this music beyond auditory perception.

I believe that the music of "the other world" is not just for the senses or the spiritual intellect of disembodied beings, nor can it be just an expression of the glorification of the Divine. I believe that it is probably the synthesis of all the harmoniously vitalized vibrations that possess an unlimited creative power on the plane where it is utilized and according to the hierarchy to which it belongs, for the purpose of an unknown transcendental evolution.

Now, as far as we on earth are concerned, these sonic illuminations are quite similar to certain mystical states of consciousness, in which the realities of the higher, ultra-terrestrial, and perhaps divine worlds manifest. Concerning music, there are certainly different spheres and planes: from the astral world to the highest planes where, perhaps, silence and sounds are one, like form and non-form, movement and statics.

These manifestations give us, for a few moments, the awareness of otherworldly realities to which human beings are called, sooner or later, to come to terms.

There is, however, a difference between these ultra-physical illuminations, which manifest themselves spontaneously (like certain mystical revelations which occur suddenly, without conscious preparation, as a testimony of divine power or grace) and other experiences where conquests are achieved through much struggle both in the mystical domain and in that of the perception of ultra-terrestrial realities through sounds, forms, or colors.

In the first case, whether in chants or supernatural instruments played in angelic fashion, these manifestations are, in general, related to some events.

In the second case, on the other hand, people can freely reach certain higher levels of consciousness by which they may experience divine worlds, in which sounds and colors are by no means excluded, but, on the contrary, manifest with a force of unimaginable beauty.

It is for their past work of receptibility and aspirations that certain beings were chosen to establish a plan of evolution. Thus, the Devic element seems particularly collaborative with them (as much as the instrument-human would allow) in the progressive realizations on the path of a music that cannot be compared to any other on earth.

But it is a fact that human beings must be prepared to be able to receive these experiences and these revelations coming from the superior worlds, for their evolution and that of the Universe.

CHAPTER TEN

~

Art and Knowledge

What is Art and what is Knowledge? Total knowledge cannot be obtained by mankind in this life. There are various paths for approaching knowledge: the scientific path, the mystical path, the philosophical path, the path of agnosticism, the path of Yoga, the path of Zen, and others. Then there is the path of Art.

This evening we will speak about the path of Art at your wishes and as simply as possible. What is Art? What is thought? What is life? Is there a definition for the essence of things?

We can only catalog works, analyze them, and more! Only those connoisseurs with courage should define what a work of art is and what is not—a judgment that is mostly impaired and affected by time and the evolution of knowledge.

But what is there to say about essence? First, that there are several forms of art—and let us admit, *a priori*, that it really is art, that is to say that the works fall into this category, without for the moment discussing them: that there is art that is testimony, popular art, folkloristic art, fantastic art, visionary art, magical art, religious art—and other forms of art as well.

Yes, there are remarkable works of art that belong to each of these categories, which shows that art is not limited to certain patterns, rules, or aesthetic doctrines.

Yes, one can detect in all valid works of art certain rules of balance and aesthetic laws which are very numerous and sometimes seem, or are, contradictory. The fact is that in reality it is very difficult to establish patterns and determine whether a work belonging to one or the other of these patterns can, therefore, be qualified as a work of art.

In reality it is extremely difficult. There are hundreds of books dealing with the problems and limitations of criticism, and on aesthetic theories that might be used to determine one's choice or judgment of values. Mountains could be made of them; but all the same, it should not be forgotten that most of the great works were unknown when they appeared—from Rembrandt or Vivaldi to our days, of all times—and before and after all the theories of aesthetics.

One needs only consider that until 1900, all African art was considered ridiculous, and that marvelous pre-Colombian gold jewelry was sold to the Bank of England for smelting because—according to some very eminent critics—it had no artistic value whatsoever. Today these gems, these works of goldsmithing are invaluable and their beauty is reputedly incomparable. This really shows the well-known limit of any aesthetic conception, and the very great limit of the most qualified critics regardless of the period.

Yes, it concerns art from other continents and the critics were Europeans; but the number of great artists who almost succumbed to starvation is very large even in Europe: painters, poets, musicians . . . that it is really not worth naming them. You should not believe that they were not known by the competent critics of their time; almost all were judged and condemned for being bad artists.

Let us take, therefore, a different point of view. I would say don't try too hard to judge the work of art—you will only get confused and make yourself look ridiculous at the next turn of history—but look instead at the creative artistic faculty of the artist and, if it is powerful and true, the work will be too. Obviously, one can judge the faculties of past artists; but there, sooner or later, time renders them justice; with contemporaries, on the other hand, it is possible that one can judge such faculties and avoid blunders, mistakes, and injustices.

Let us say: creative artistic faculty. What is it?

It is the ability to arrest motion, to crystallize an instant of duration, to tear it from oneself—and to project this instant through an effort of the entire being, in a verbal, sonic, or plastic matter.

This is really the best definition. However, there is also another possibility, another method of creation, it consists of transmitting movement and duration not by an effort of one's entire being, but, on the contrary, by the most complete submission to this duration and movement in which one participates, traverses, and fills it. This second method is the one generally adopted by Asian artists.

Yes, that is it. It is a bit like natural childbirth and painless childbirth. But for the second, you know, you need a particular sort of technique, a preparation, not to mention, for example anesthesia, which could, in turn, correspond more or less to the trance of a medium. In painless childbirth, consciousness remains present, but it is accomplished without the pangs, the cries, and the dramas that accompany natural childbirth. Yes, it is somewhat like that. But all the comparisons are always very approximate, and I use them—as well as analogies and examples—only very little and unwillingly.

Yes, what the essence of art is is still not very clear, of course, but it will become somewhat clear as you listen to me: the answer is not so simple.

I told you that the creative faculty was the crystallization of an instant of duration and its outward projection by the artist. This is already something, unless we want to define, now, what is duration, movement, and everything that creates the phenomenology of the universe and its life are. But I will tell you again, with another very approximate and not very relevant analogy, that just as there is not the disease but the patient, there is not the art but the artist. Patients live if they get rid of death, artists die if they do not give birth to life.

We must, therefore, return from the object of art to its creator. (I use the word "creator" here to simplify things. I will tell you later that this word is not relevant and that in reality nobody creates anything. For the moment, I will continue to say that the artist creates and to speak of creative faculty, in order not to complicate the argument, which is very complex.) Therefore, to consider the artist independent of the artwork, which can be placed in any historical period or moment of aesthetic evolutions created under any nationalistic or foreign influence of groups or individuals, we must consider the artist on his own merit, with his own faculties, and the artwork more as the outcome of the creative faculties of this artist.

Yes, how can we analyze the creative faculties of artists, living or dead?

For dead artists it is more difficult; but I find that traditional criticism can no longer rely too much on its own criteria. Should an Egyptian or Khmer sculpture, a Ming or Tang object be considered according to the time and period in which it was created, under which emperor, and judged according to its genealogy, so to speak, the family to which it belonged—or should it be judged in itself? Would it be less beautiful if we knew that it had been produced under the reign of the next or previous emperor, a hundred years before or after, or under completely different historical conditions and aesthetic influences? Or even, if we absolutely did not know to which era it belongs? No, it is the intrinsic quality of the object, of the work, which only counts, that is to say the "result," the "manifestation" of the particular faculties of the creative artist.

The work of art is valid only in relation to this extraordinary experience of effort of crystallization of movement, of duration, by the artist and its projection into the material, even independently, in part, of the "content" of the movement perceived at such a moment in history, or of the historical and geographical position of the artist within human society.

Yes, of course: It is difficult to isolate the artist from his milieu. We know too well what the artist's place is in a corner of the world, at a point in history—especially in the history that we understand, which is the city where he learned his craft, who his teachers or his contemporaries were—the artist cannot be isolated from all that. Everything that preceded him and that surrounded him determines a historical vision of his creation and his works. In reality, however, we can clearly see that time is responsible for disengaging part of all this, because the possible ignorance of all these factors does not in any way eliminate the true essential quality of the work which proceeds from all other fundamental elements of the artist.

But enough said. You asked me what art is. I have given you a definition which I believe to be the best and the most accurate, but for all art and all works of art there are no absolutes. There is no absolute definition of art just as there is none of life. But I tell you once again, that the work of art results from certain psychophysical operations specific to the creative artist, which allow him to halt the course of duration and to project an instant of it into any matter whatsoever. If the artist is not able to accomplish this, he is not such an individual and the resulting work might be anything but art. It could be a piece of craftsmanship, something academic, a work of deception, of exploitation, of plagiarism—any of these—but not art.

Perhaps I am letting myself get a bit carried away with a polemic vis-à-vis the current and classic theories regarding works of art. Evidently, the critics are partly correct. But as I already said, they do not take into account other factors which, in my opinion, are more essential. I let myself be dragged maybe a bit too much into a polemic about current and classic theories regarding works of art. Obviously, critics are partially right; but, like I already said, they don't reckon with other factors that, in my opinion, are more essential.

Nevertheless, polemics are always to be avoided. An idea, a new or different concept must be self-assertive and established itself with evidence. It is not necessary, then, to attack other ideas, which are sometimes complementary anyway.

I am strongly opposed to any theory supporting the idea that you must wipe the ground clean first; a good practice, which is very often applied, unfortunately. This destruction—this clearing—is immediately considered a new contribution, a new idea, whereas in reality, most likely, this action stops there as an end in itself. What is destroyed is replaced by nothing. An idea not replaced by another, except by the very idea of destruction, is not an idea at all.

Certain aesthetic movements have introduced some new and interesting ideas. Take Surrealism, for example. What has remained of this movement sometimes is still quite alive. It is not the polemic, the violent attack on society, but a certain aesthetic contribution which results from a new conception of artistic creation.

The rejection of reason, not only discursive and logical but in its entirety, constitutes this movement's essential character which separates it from the others.

With Surrealism, creation ultimately strives for man's conquest of the infinite through the powers of not-reasoning, of irrationality and automatic writing; hence, by its psychic automatism it is completely protected against any intervention by the intellect. This is the goal to which surrealistic poetry and all works of art must aim according to what Breton asserted in his first manifesto. In essence, it was taking Baudelaire's famous "vaporization" to the limit—a term that contrasts with concentration.

This formula, of course, called for very great ambitions, for it went beyond all aesthetics and even tended toward a sort of revelation of powers present in the human unconscious as linked to cosmic wholeness; but obviously, in this automatism, in this "vaporization," forces of any order, of any kind, can manifest themselves. Powers of any order and kind can manifest itself in this automatism. Baudelaire had already said it: "Through this wide-open door can enter both angels and demons."

No, I do not believe that the Surrealists achieved their goal. In poetry and literature, despite certain accounts of Breton, Desnos, Soupault, Leiris, and others, they did not go beyond the superficial layers of dreams and the unconscious. They lacked a more profound psychological technique to reach states of consciousness in a different order of time and space. In painting, they lacked an additional graphic dimension that would have enabled them to represent motion and dream. They remain in the traditional dimension, anachronistic and devoid of meaning. To depict dreams and certain connections through a type of association capable to express the unconscious and motion, it would have required a four-dimensional graphic perspective.

Yes, the Dadaists also attacked society, and everything else, but what remains of that is the idea of a dislocation of logical discourse carried to its extreme consequences, as well as the idea of constantly free action elevated to principle of art.

The revolt against past and present—or the established order—does not concern art at all. We may say the same about certain demagogic aesthetic movements.

As spectacles, or as works, there were some amusing gags in which certain minds can take pleasure, but also a certain masochism, a desire for destruction, or self-destruct. I must add, however, that Surrealists and Dadaists, unknowingly or perhaps not, blindfolded by their revolt and without the means to achieve it, longed for something deeper and larger than themselves.

I think that this could be a subject for study, because many violent acts, destruction, and self-destruction stem from an unconscious but powerful desire, from an inner need to break through a wall, to break out of oneself, from one's prison, without knowing how or being able to succeed. Not knowing how to achieve this, we break everything around us, or we commit suicide.

Yes, of course, art is not made of ideas, but I said that some worthwhile works were generated by these ideas—and even then, they were not really ideas. We define them as an afterthought, but that is not correct; they are experiences that arise at a certain level of consciousness, and of which one becomes aware. If one might speak of a "new box" that illuminates the self. Yes, don't laugh, man is made of boxes and drawers, he is full of boxes by the hundreds, by the thousands. A good number have been open, illuminated for a long time, millennia; but all the time others are opening and illuminating and then mankind becomes aware of their content. The content becomes obvious to him. Sometimes he does not comprehend it immediately, he does not really know what it is; he cannot identify it because it is a question of something new and this novelty upsets other things; he is forced to tear or establish relationships, to modify them, to accept changes in his thought patterns or in life, and this does not happen without confusion—of course.

However, there is nothing one can do. When a box is opened, its contents even take priority for a while, until a new box lights up, and the process begins again eternally.

Do you want to know how these boxes are illuminated or opened? Ah, well! It is a long story that begins with the perception of interior and exterior phenomena and ends, for the artist, when he finishes with a work of art. We will return to this later.

Yes, I believe that the problems are the same in all the arts. There is sometimes a time lag between the appearance of the problem and the solution, faster or slower, in one or the other forms of art. But in fact, under the influence of continental and intercontinental communications such as radio, magazines, exhibitions, concerts, conferences, and travels by the artists to different countries, the problems arise practically parallel and at the same time for all.

It is interesting to note, for instance, the parallel and progressive disappearance of the subject in painting and the theme in music. Or the concept of equivalence (positive and negative space) in painting and the equal importance of the note and of rest (emptiness and fullness). This leads to the concept of integrated space, or the white or black surface in painting, and silence in music. Or even the concept of collage, where everything is combined: newspapers, posters, advertisements, clippings of naked people, and landscapes. In music, street noises, radio, bits of melody, words, and machine noises are combined or superimposed.

Certainly, in painting one can observe the almost complete disappearance of color, replaced by paper, rags, scorched iron, scraped or torn sheet-metal, or also by nails, toothbrushes, and even pieces of hygienic utensils.

Equally in music, the disappearance of the melodic or harmonic interval, replaced by strings that are beaten, struck, filed, and scraped with tools or more unusual objects. Even the woods of the instruments are treated in a way that is sometimes appalling from the point of view of their conservation—when one does not want to destroy them on purpose, as it happened to certain pianos during a "music" *séance* that has remained rather famous.

It is the same way in poetry. The same problems and the same types of solutions: spatial graphic, typographic, and so on. I would not want to continue this, but the world knows what it is about certain texts.

This is a very interesting parallel that I researched at one time, and that belonged to a study that probably will never be completed. Part of the manuscript was stolen from me in Paris. It was in a suitcase full of documents, music manuscripts, and books inscribed by Michaux, Reverdy, Jouve, and other friends, poets, and writers. The suitcase was found in very good condition, but its content perished in the Seine—I am sure of it—unless the thief was a collector of autographs. They were souvenirs of my life in Paris, but in the end, in one way or another, souvenirs always end up in the ocean of oblivion.

Yes, why are the problems the same and practically concurrent in all the arts? This is not easy to say, but as I tried to explain, the artist effects a process of crystallization of movement, which is perceived by all artists and projected by each one into the material that suits their psychophysical organism and faculties.

Yes, I understand very well that in the life of a human being, of an artist, very different things happen, things very different from those that happen in the life of another. Hence, each artist can crystallize and project elements of very different movement and must face a nearly infinite endless variety of problems and solutions. Yes, but it is not. We say that certain things are in the air, but this is a rather vague way of expressing a reality.

The concomitance of certain discoveries, of certain manifestations, is not due to chance. Rather it is due to the faculties of the artists' perception who, at a particular moment, synthesize the frequency of certain wavelengths and, at the same time, the quality of these waves, which are suddenly recorded very intensively by an extremely large number of people.

I could offer numerous examples of works that evince parallel aesthetic inquiry in the different arts during the same era and in a single country. But even more surprising are examples of the appearance of artistic expressions that yield the same tendency, such that similar designs and symbols appear concurrently in different countries and even in distant continents. It has been this way since antiquity.

In part this involves art history; I have just dealt with many such works, encyclopedias, and so on. But there are also passionate hypotheses concerning the evolution of mankind, society, and the world that perhaps we can take up another time.

Why are the faculties of artists synthesized at the same moment in a way that is nearly identical, and what is this quality of frequencies—or content of motion—that can be recorded so intensely everywhere at the same moment?

Ah well, we have entered another domain that really belongs to the origin of art, to be sure, but which no longer has anything to do with either criticism or aesthetics . . . the discourse would become quite lengthy—the one about the boxes, indeed. It will be something for another time.

There is in man—apart from the Soul—the monad, the spirit, the atman, or whatever you wish to call that which is intransient in mankind, and which survives throughout his lives. It has four fundamental elements:

1. The Vital Element—which has a rhythmic character in its physiological manifestations. Rhythms that go from simple to very complex, that are sometimes measurable only with very complex diagrams or electronic instruments, such as cellular rhythms of thought, the emotions, the senses, and so on.
2. The Emotional Element—which includes all categories of what we call sentiment. These are products of experiences in the purely emotional realm, or of those in the vital physical element, or those that may be called psychic.
3. The Psychic Element—which is very difficult to delimit and to define, and which includes all experiences stemming from the intuitive domain, the subconscious, the dream, the superconscious, clairvoyance, and even mystical enlightenment.
4. The Intellectual Element—which is the rational part, the superior intellect that is closer to the psychic element—and which includes the will and memory.

Clearly these four elements are not insulated compartments, keeping each one from participating in the manifestation of the others. So, it is not emotional, psychic, or intellectual manifestation that would be impossible if the vital element were absent and vice versa. Similarly, all psychic or sensorial elements create emotional states that belong to the emotional realm, and so on.

There are certainly experiences that one could call total, in which all the elements participate with maximum of intensity. In this case, it is virtually impossible to determine the respective importance of each affected element, for the inter-penetration of the elements nearly produces absolute fusion in the consciousness.

Yes, but if total experience exists, there are others in which one only element seems to dominate, or to be directly affected, or that may exist independently of the others, taking into account the psychophysical unity of mankind. It would really take too long to list all possible examples of these mutual relationships that occur with the experiences that our perceptions pass to the consciousness.

Yes, but what is consciousness? It is very difficult to define because consciousness involves both the physical and the nonphysical.

What can I tell you briefly? Consciousness is a living reality that reacts to all physical and nonphysical impressions, and thus undergoes continuous modification.

All theory that considers just the physical element of consciousness cannot account for the sum of its manifestations. If an organic or functional alteration of the human organism reduces its faculties, [then] a psychic change produces the same result. On the other hand, if certain cerebral localization constitutes the material pole of consciousness, the opposite pole—or the immaterial element—while not localized, is no less present, nevertheless.

It must be said that it is not only the perception that any state is produced in the consciousness, and here we could speak of the theory of engrams and so on—which would carry us much too far—as also different theories of perception; but also all perceived experiences belong to one or the other of the four elements that we have called *fundamental*.

All this could definitely be developed further. Piles of books exist, all sorts of works that address these issues. I must discuss this briefly here perhaps with some inaccuracies, for I want to return as quickly as possible to the artist/human being. However, there is still something else that should be mentioned: namely the identification faculty. Without this, all interior or exterior experiences, whether they belong to one category or the other, would remain vague and indefinite in the consciousness. These states that we occasionally feel are difficult to define and can hardly imagine lasting for a long time, for the faculty of identification intervenes as soon as possible.

It is also difficult to say what [the identification faculty] consists of, because of its irreducible character. One can only say that it does not proceed exclusively through the mechanism of association, nor it is that mechanism itself.

It is likely that the establishment of a relationship as a means of identification is something different from purely rational abstraction, and that the act of identification does perceive the essence of this relationship, which means that it possesses—or implies—real qualities of cognition.

Identification appears to be a real tool for a vital and immediate recognition, a close relationship with the intellect. We can therefore consider the states of consciousness produced by different perceptions as able of transiting at any instant from the unknown field into the known—that is to say, constituting virtual images.

Now we may return to the last question that we posed earlier, which is: Why are the perceptive faculties of artists synthesized at the same moment in (almost) the same way, capturing certain categories and certain qualities of perception? And why do certain artistic experiences manifest in more or less the same way, and more or less at the same time? Why is this so? Well! The reasons are many.

First, there are cycles, which occur in everything. In the life of mankind, these four fundamental elements which condition the faculty of perception and vary in activity according to the course not only of its life but also of a single day.

Yes, the faculty of identification of perceptions also appears to vary in intensity and in clarity following its own laws, which seem to be conditioned primarily by the character of the perceptions—that is, principally by those of the psychic order. For as seen at the time, the faculty of identification involves both the physical and the nonphysical, and through the nonphysical aspect, it is therefore one of the faculties of humans that, more than others, connects them to the highest cosmic forces.

Finally, it is this faculty that links the artist as well as the mystic, in different ways, to the realm which we call *supernatural* and which only becomes conscious, appears to our consciousness, when it is identified, clarified, and known in the proportions or limits of the possible.

How does all this concern the artist more than other human being? You are right, everything I have said is common to all people. What then is the difference with the artist?

What differentiates the creative artist (let us call him that, even if the term is not exact) from the individual who is not resides less in the quality or variety of the states of consciousness and images than in the creative artist's desire and capacity to project out of himself and to crystallize, as I said, in a sonorous, verbal, or plastic matter.

It is indeed this desire and this capacity which imply a particular nature and activity of certain functions and certain capacities that place special value on the experiences themselves, their crystallization, and their sensory manifestation.

It would take much too long to analyze what this capacity involves. I would say that all intellectual, emotional, or physical faculties—whether muscular or intellectual—requires an activity. The psychophysical conditioning of the artist is such that his four elements are suited to a particular activity and crave it. This desire is a natural dynamic impulse geared for its own manifestation.

Similarly, the artist's faculty of identification tends to be applied more intensely to certain experiences, or states of consciousness, which are linked to the desires and to the activity of certain of his faculties. Again, this seems difficult to understand, but in reality, it is not as abstruse as it appears.

As I said, by the very nature of the faculty of identification, the experiences and images result from a large part of "cognition," and thus of meaning and sensory content. This is how we can speak of poetry, or of art, as a means of knowledge. The peculiar value that one attributes to works of art, to artistic creations, stem precisely from the fact that they are the visible crystallization and the material incarnation of a process of direct and unique knowledge of creative cosmic forces.

But there is even more. If, on the other hand, the artist arrives at this cognitive contact through creative forces, there is also an activity of these very same [creative] forces that impact the human organism and in particular the artist.

The entire organism of the artist is made, so to speak, to receive and to collect—and desires to do so. Everything is open to him and he receives and collects everything that interests him and is within reach. But if he is conditioned to do this, it is because he was conditioned by complex processes and by physical and spiritual nature since birth, in life, and, I believe, probably also through the course of a long, prior evolution.

The forces use this conditioned organism for their own goals that are beyond us, but we must serve these goals because we are, in sum, conditioned by them.

We do not deprive our muscles of exercises, our legs to walk, or our brain to think, unless we act against nature and this would result in unfortunate consequences for us. The same is true with respect to these higher activities that are just as draconian.

We do not know why we exist—or at least the search for such knowledge falls outside tonight's topic—but we do know that all people must do something, that their own organism must act one way or another, according to a law of nature. One must exercise; one must work; one must function. If according to one's will or the will of others, one prevents or refuses action, or one is restricted, or one denies this functioning, it is either suicide or homicide.

So, all human organisms must function, exercise, and work—whether for better or for worse, that is another question—but it must function.

What is the purpose of all this work? This question relates to one about existence. There is a purpose because the theory of chance is really insufficient. The purpose of the artist—as I said at the beginning—is the purpose of these faculties: to crystallize an instance of duration and to project it onto matter. This purpose transcends technical work and its ability. For if the artist were restricted by technique, he would be like any other conscientious craftsman, but he would be unaware of these particular faculties that allow him to get in contact with the plans and forces that transcend him and that only he can manifest.

The manifestation of these forces, which through the artist influence the world, has a purpose that we can only imagine or glimpse.

The power of artistic radiance and vibration on the human and collective psyche is indisputably enormous, greater than we suppose, in the general economy of cosmic forces, for the evolution of the planet and human thought.

It is search and asceticism—if you will—whose goal must be not conquest but surrender and submission. Surrender and submission then turn into victory preceded, however, by humility and un-selflessness.

Yes, this may be considered asceticism. The work of art is the fruit of a hypersensitive creative intuition, which one reaches progressively if one does not have the good chance of being one of those "elected."

Thus, for the artist it is a matter of research. It is at the higher spectra of vibrations and knowledge that the artist must refine his faculties of perception and identification, and [he must] work humbly at the service of the same faculties that conditioned him, for it is the most marvelous task ever given to a living being to accomplish on this earth. And now listen, for as long as you can hear it, to the resonance of the harmonics of this deep note.

Conclusion

Cercles (1986) and Octologo (1987) as Manifestations of Post "Late Style"

Most Scelsi scholars agree on the division of the composer's creative styles into three periods: (1) the traditional or historical phase that concluded, in 1949, with *La nascita del verbo*; (2) the transitional or esoteric stylistic current that included a large corpus of mostly piano music influenced by Hindu-Buddhist traditions that ended before 1959; (3) the microtonal search for the depth of sound as an elusive third dimension, which aligned Scelsi with the most influential figures in twentieth-century music when *Quattro pezzi per orchestra (ciascuno su una sola nota)* (1959) took the musical avantgarde world by storm. It propelled Scelsi as a strong creative force.

The microtonal style petered out, though, when Vieri Tosatti—the Roman composer who helped Scelsi transform his myriad ondiola taped improvisations into the works the world learned to appreciate—severed his long-standing collaboration. In fact, Tosatti's assistance was no longer needed since Scelsi's major works had begun to travel around the globe escorted by the composer when his health permitted. It was then that Scelsi entered a post "Late Style," a time for reflection about his troubled creativity too often intertwined with the conflicts generated by his unmethodical search for the transformation of an inner self. That transformation fully emerged in 1959 through the crystallization of a single sound, *una nota sola*, its disintegration into infinite particles, and its re-integration into an unscientific spherical sonic construct.

Rather than Adorno's much-discussed concept of Late Style in Beethoven's case, the philosophical thinking imbued in Scelsi's last period was closer to Edward Said's complex view of "exile" that saw the creative individual encircling the globe—and indeed the universe—in search of a legacy to bestow upon posterity. Ultimately, Giacinto Scelsi found his place by capturing the celestial "hum" that fascinated so many "visionary listeners" since the time of Plato.

Although one may claim that the career of Giacinto Scelsi, the mythic *homme du son*, began in the early 1960s, it reached its conclusion in August (08) – (08) – 1988, at his house in Rome's Via S. Teodoro 8 where a fatal cardiac crisis claimed his life early the next day. Giacinto Scelsi was born on January 8, 1905.

The number eight and its symbolic meanings were fundamental to Scelsi's concepts of infinity and eternity and core in his thinking. So, as he neared his earthly departure, he felt compelled to pen *Cercles* (Circles) and *Octologo* (Octologue) for his followers to reflect upon. Let us observe the *Octologo* first.

Octologo is a document translated into eight languages listing eight aphorisms. It was published by Luciano Martinis in a limited edition of 323 copies on Scelsi's birthday falling on January 8 (1987). It read like a synthetic expression of his life.

1.
Do not become opaque
nor allow the others
to opaque you

2.
Do not think
leave the thinking
to those who have need of thinking

3.
Detachement
not renounciation

4.
Aspire to everything
want nothing

5.
Between man and woman
union not joining

6.
Make Art
without art

7.
You are the children and the parents of yourselves;
do not forget it

8.
Do not diminish
the sense which
you do not understand

Commandments, precepts, aphorisms, maxims, confessions, and the like have rained upon mankind since the beginning of time. Scholars glossed over them with a flood of words to fit any ideological value or state of mind. Such is not the case with Scelsi. His expression *una nota sola* (just one note) applied to his late music, corresponds to *una parola sola* (just one word), which resonates well when pondering the *Octologo*.

The process of crystallization leading to the aesthetic of *una nota sola, una parola sola* also extended to Scelsi's poetic output, particularly in *Cercles* (Circles), his last collection of poems published in June 1986 by *Le parole gelate* as a slender, elegant, austere short book whose refined cardboard cover bore the drawing of a circle symbolizing the poetic essence contained in a few gestures; from verbal matter to graphic sign, from words to geometrical shapes in progressive evolution.

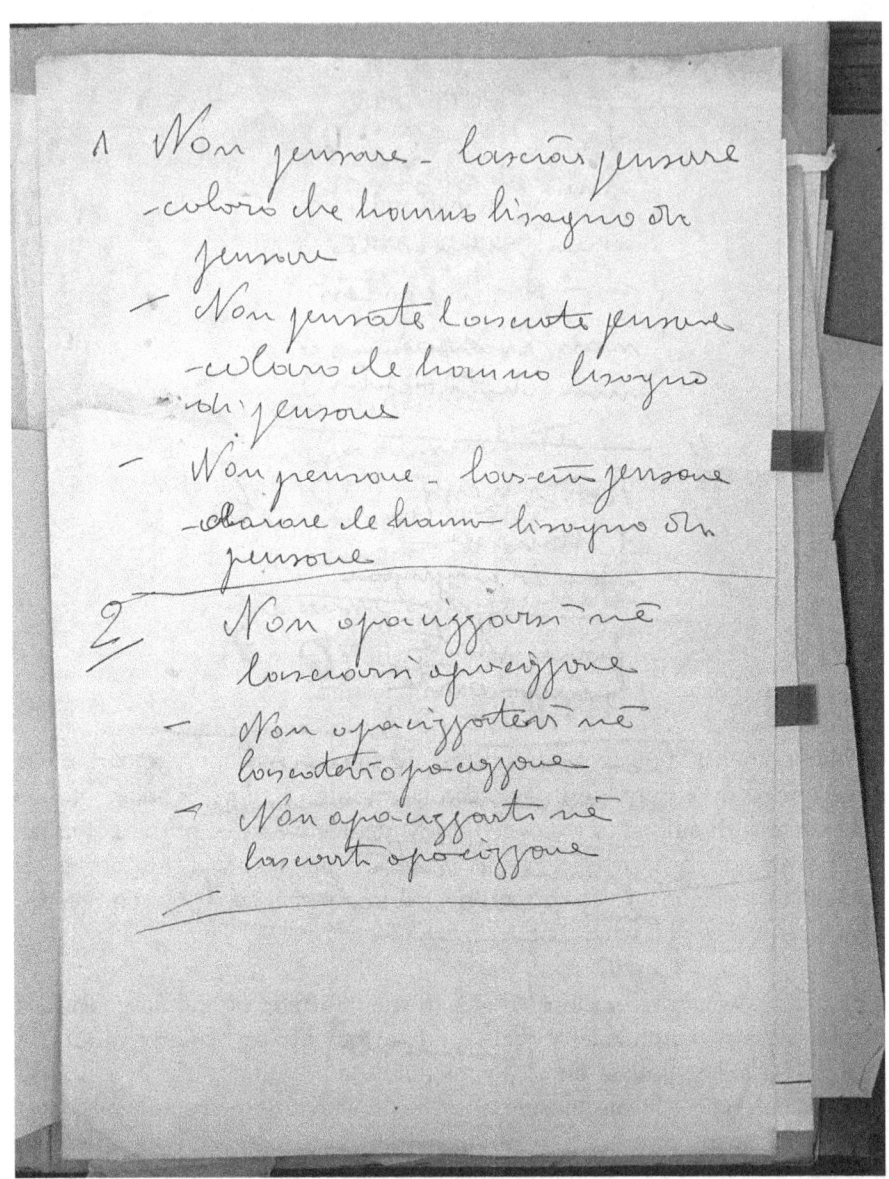

Figure 11.1. Scelsi's autographed sketch of *Octologo*. Page 1.
© Fondazione Isabella Scelsi. Roma

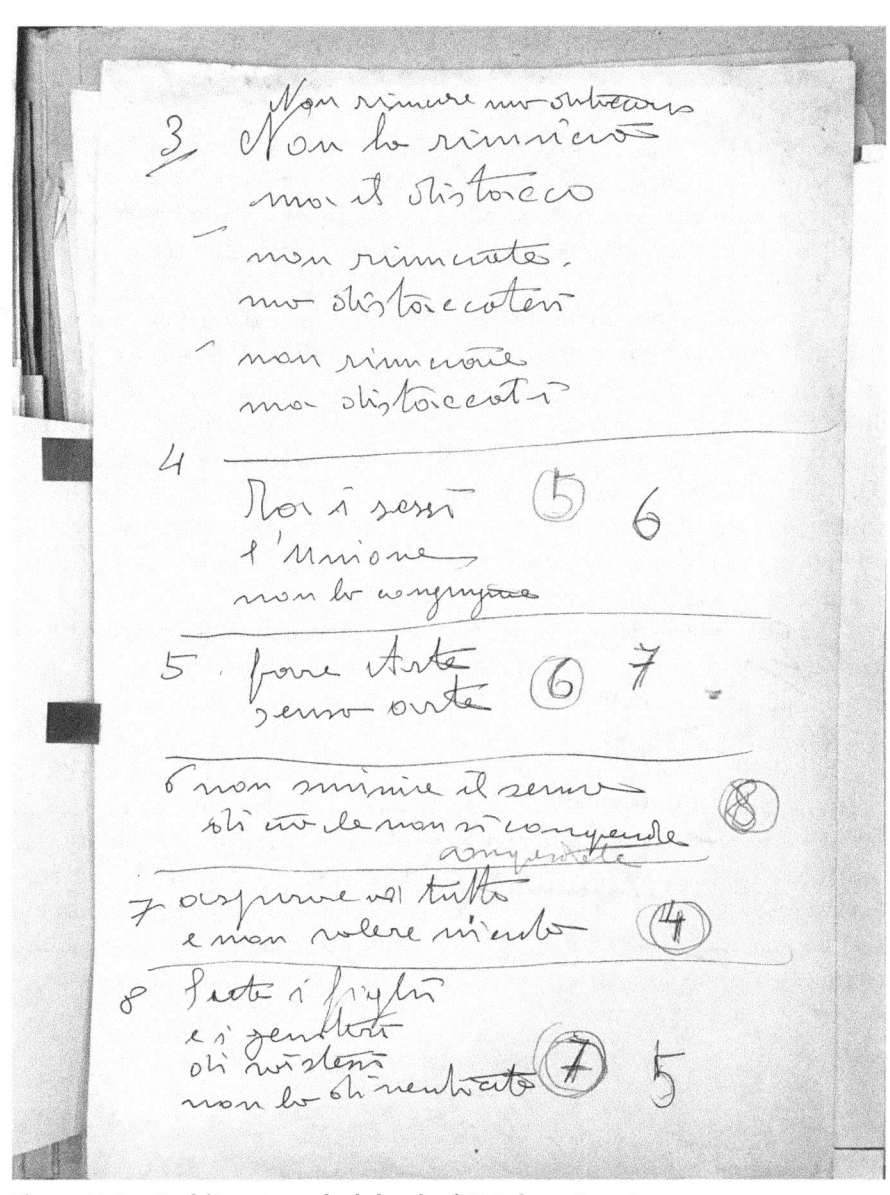

Figure 11.2. Scelsi's autographed sketch of *Octologo*. Page 2.
© Fondazione Isabella Scelsi. Roma

These dense poems, expressed in concise verses, contract themselves gradually to the point of becoming a word—just one word sufficient to enliven a full page. Then, geometrical shapes—also placed each on a single page—represent their transformation from triangle to pentagon, hexagon, octagon, decagon, dodecagon, and ultimately to a circle.[1]

The verbal flow, once ossified in the geometry of the signs, reemerges to conclude the collection of poems with a few last aphoristic verses.

In 1982, Scelsi's oneiric narrative about his existence found an early expression in *Il sogno 101—Il ritorno* (The Dream 101—The Comeback), the second part of an autobiography originally penned in Italian, which consisted of an initial, ampler text written in prose form and a more concise one written in verses. The latter saw the light in 1982 under Scelsi's eyes as a small book published by *Le parole gelate*. It dealt with a dreamy vision of his own life in which elements of nature like the rustle of leaves intersect with innumerable references to the cosmos and to the vibratory essence of sound, its sphericity, transparence, and luminosity.

Geometric shapes also recur in his full autobiographical account—like a *leitmotiv* in gradual evolution as the role of the book's narrator, cast in first person, materializes in geometric figures until he becomes a circle, a great circle of light end energy.[2]

The parallel between the autobiographical *Il ritorno* and the last book of poems, *Cercles*, is surprisingly consequential. In fact, it is already revealed in Scelsi's writings collected in the present volume. It is transfiguration distilled into poetic matter; the process of aphoristic abstraction that characterizes Scelsi's late style having now reached its pinnacle and sealed by the drawing that became universally known as his symbol and signature: the line and the circle.

Figure 11.3. Scelsi's *Circle and Line* autographed signature.
© Fondazione Isabella Scelsi. Roma

Scelsi himself explained this choice in a letter to a friend. He wrote:

"[. . .] ce dessin [. . .] qui est mon symbol et qui me représente. Il peut être interprété comme un sign Zen, ou comme le Soleil sur l'horizon, ou également comme un grand Zéro souligné. Comme on veut!"[3]

Notes

1. Giacinto Scelsi. *Cercles*, Roma, le parole gelate, 1986, 28–36. Also see Giacinto Scelsi, *L'homme du son. Poésies recuellies et commentés par Luciano Martinis, avec la collaboration de Sharon Kanach*, Arles, Actes Sud, 2006, 231–239.

2. "Sono un triangolo o devo cambiare forma?/ Prendere un ['] altra forma/Sento che posso prendere qualunque forma/ E diventare largo o stretto./ No, resto triangolo."
(Am I a triangle or must I change my shape? / Assuming another shape / I feel I can assume any shape / And becoming large or narrow. / No, I shall remain a triangle.)
See Giacinto Scelsi, *Il sogno 101 – Il ritorno*, Roma, le parole gelate, 1982, 20. Also Giacinto Scelsi, *Il sogno 101*, a cura di Luciano Martinis e Alessandra Carlotta Pellegrini, Macerata: Quodlibet, 2010, 399.

3. Giacinto Scelsi, [Lettre a Mme Mollia], in *Les anges sont ailleurs . . . Textes et inédits recueillis et commentés par Sharon Kanach*, Arles: Actes Sud, 2006, 30.

Bibliography

Allen, Roger. *Richard Wagner's Beethoven (1870): A New Translation*. Woodbridge: Boydell & Brewer, 2014.

Beausire, Pierre. *Essai sue la poèsie et la poetique de Mallarmè*. Lausanne: Roth, 1942.

Bergson, Henry. *L'Évolution créatrice*. Paris: Alcan, 1907.

Boyle, Katie. *What This Katie Did: An Autobiography*. London: Weidenfield and Nicolson, 1980.

Castanet, Pierre-Albert e Nicola Cisternino (a cura). *Giacinto Scelsi: Viaggio al centro del suono*. La Spezia: Luna Editore, 1993. Second Edition, 2001.

Cremonese, Adriano. "A proposito di due inedita di Giacinto Scelsi" in *i suoni, le onde…Rivista della Fondazione Isabella Scelsi* 2, 1991: 14-18.

——— (a cura). "Giacinto Scelsi" in *Musik-Konzepte 31*. Roma: Le parole gelate, 1985.

——— (a cura). *Évolution de l'harmonie* (Evoluzione dell'armonia). Roma: Fondazione Isabella Scelsi, 1992.

——— (a cura). *Évolution du rythme* (Evoluzione del ritmo). Roma: Fondazione Isabella Scelsi, 1992.

Féron, François-Xavier. "Les variations dans la vibration: vibrato, tremolos et trilles dans la Trilogie—*Les trois stades de l'homme (1956–1965) pour violoncelle seul de Giacinto Scelsi*," in "Scelsi incombustible," *Filigrane*, n. 15, Maggio 2012 (monographic issue edited by Makis Solomos and Alessandra Carlotta Pellegrini, available at [httpa://revues.mshparisnord.fr/filigrane/index.php?id=516] accessed 5 June 2022.

Fontainas, André. *Mes Souvenirs du Symbolism*. Paris: Éditions de la Nouvelle Revue Critique, 1928.

Hasler, Alfred A. *The Lifeboat Is Full: Switzerland and the Refugees, 1933–1945*. New York: Funk & Wagnalls, 1969.
Jaecker, Friedrich (Ed.). *Giacinto Scelsi. Die Magie des Klangs—Gesammelte Schriften*, 2 vols. Köln: Edition Musik Text, 2013.
Kanach, Sharon (Ed.). *Giacinto Scelsi. Les anges sont ailleurs . . . Textes et inédits recuillis et commentés par Sharon Kanach*. Arles: Actes Sud, 2006.
Metzger, Heinz-Klaus, and Rainer Riehn (Eds.). *Musik-Konzept 31—Giacinto Scelsi*: München: Edition Text & Kritik, 1983. Second edition enlarged and updated, 2015.
Pellegrini, Carlotta Alessandra, and Franco Sciannameo (Eds.). *Music as Dream: Essays on Giacinto Scelsi*: Lanham: Scarecrow Press, 2013.
Ramsden, Dorothy Kate. *Randolph's Folly*. London: Sampson Low, Marston & Company, 1945.
Said, Edward W. *On Late Style*. London: Bloomsbury Publishing, 2006.
Scelsi, Giacinto. *Il sogno 101* (a cura). Luciano Martinis e Alessandra Carlotta Pellegrini. Macerata: Quodlibet, 2010.
Schaeffner, André. *Strawinsky*. Paris: Les Éditions Rieder, 1931.
Sciannameo, Franco, and Alessandra Carlotta Pellegrini (Eds.). *Music as Dream: Essays on Giacinto Scelsi*: Lanham, MD: Scarecrow Press, 2013.
Steiner, Rudolf. *L'essenza della musica e l'esperienza del suono nell'uomo*. Translation by Dante Vigevani. Milano: Editrice Antroposofica, 1973.
———. *L'initiation: ou Comment acquérir des connaissances sur les modes supérieurs*. Translated by Maria Steiner. Paris: La science spirituelle, 1948.
Swan, Alfred Julius. *Scriabin*. London: John Lane, 1923.
Thibodeau, Norman C. "Richard Falk and His Performing Adaptations of Eighteenth-Century Opera." Unpublished Master Essay. Baltimore: The Peabody Institute of The John Hopkins University, 1990.
Toniutti, Agnese. "Randolph's Folly. Un romanzo di Dorothy Kate Ramsden" *in i suoni, le onde . . . Rivista della Fondazione Isabella Scelsi* 16, 2006: 10–13.

Discography

1972–2022

Simone Caputo

The discography of Giacinto Scelsi is divided in two sections: "Dedicated Recordings" and "Collections." The former presents the music albums entirely dedicated to works by Scelsi, while the latter lists miscellaneous music collections containing just one or more works by Scelsi. The records are arranged following an ascending chronological order. The titles of the works are reported as indicated on each music album. The main sources used to compile the discography follow.

Archivio della Fondazione Isabella Scelsi
I suoni, le onde . . . : Rivista della Fondazione Isabella Scelsi
Giacinto Scelsi 1905–1988 (catalogue des éditions Salabert, 2005),
    discography edited by Sharon Kanach and Fabio Carboni
Scelsi: Discography, edited by Todd M. McComb, http://www.medieval
    .org/music/modern/scelsi/discs.html
Online catalogs of record labels, discographic databases

Dedicated Recordings
1978
Hô - Khoom - Pranam
Michiko Hirayama
Ananda, LP, 3

1980
Giacinto Scelsi. Sauh, Taiagarú, Canti del Capricorno
Michiko Hirayama
Ananda, LP, 5

1982
Giacinto Scelsi. Quattro pezzi, Pranam II, Okanagon, Kya
Ensemble 2E2M, Luca Pfaff
FY, LP, FY103

1983
Giacinto Scelsi. Paralipomena 2, Quartets and Duos
The Arditti String Quartet
Fore, 2 LP, FORE 80/THIRTEEN FOURTEEN

1985
Giacinto Scelsi. Musique Sacrée
Groupe Vocal de France, John Patrick Thomas, Eric Lundquist
FY, LP, FY 119

1988
Giacinto Scelsi. Aiôn, Pfhat, Konx-Om-Pax
Orchestre et Chœur de la Radio-Télévision Polonaise de Cracovie, Jürg Wyttenbach
Accord, CD, 200402
Giacinto Scelsi. Dodici preludi, Poemi, Variazioni e fuga
Giuseppe Scotese
EdiPan/La Musica, CD (distributed with the magazine La Musica), n. 17
Giacinto Scelsi. Ka and Ttai

Marianne Schroeder
hat ART, CD, hat ART CD 6006

1989

Giacinto Scelsi
[Triphon, Three Latin Prayers, Pranam II, Antifona, In nome lucis I, Tre canti sacri, In nommine lucis V]
Ensemble 2e2m, Luca Pfaff, David Simpson, Eric Lundquist et al.
Disques Fy et du Solstice, CD, FYCD 119

Giacinto Scelsi. Elegia per Ty, Divertimento no. 3 pour violon, L'Âme Ailée, L'Âme Ouverte, Coelocanth, Trio a cordes
Robert Zimansky, Christoph Schiller, Patrick Demenga
Accord, CD, 200622

Giacinto Scelsi. Quattro pezzi per orchestra, Anahit, Uaxuctum
Orchestre et Chœur de la Radio-Télévision Polonaise de Cracovie, with Jürg Wyttenbach, Carmen Fournier, Tristan Murail et al.
Accord, CD, 200612

Musikprotokoll '89: Giacinto Scelsi. Hymnos, Riti (I funerali d'Achille), Canti del Capricorno, Rucke di Guck
ORF-Symphonieorchester, Hans Zender, Michiko Hirayama et al.
ORF, CD, 1989

1990

Giacinto Scelsi. Quattro illustrazioni, Xnoybis, Cinque incantesimi, Duo pour violon et violoncelle
Suzanne Fournier, Carmen Fournier, David Simpson
Accord, CD, 200742

Scelsi: 1905–1988
[Kya, Ixor, Ko Lho, Maknongan, Fleuve magicue, Arc en ciel, Pwyll, Pranam, Quattro pezzi, Aitsi]
Ensemble 2E2M, with Paul Méfano
Adda, CD, 581189 (reissue of Adda, 243112, CD, 1990)

1991

Giacinto Scelsi. Suite no. 8, "Bot-Ba" (Tibet); Suite no. 9, "Ttai" (Paix)
Werner Bärtschi
Accord, CD, 200802

1992
Giacinto Scelsi. Bot-Ba
Marianne Schroeder
hat ART, CD, hat ART CD 6092

Giacinto Scelsi. Tre Canti Popolari
Helix Ensemble, Vincent Bouchot, Paul Gérimon, Lucy Grauman,
   Marianne Pousseur et al.
Sub Rosa, CD, SR51

1993
Giacinto Scelsi. Okanagon
Joëlle Léandre
hat ART, CD, hat ART CD 6124

Giacinto Scelsi
[Pranam, Ko-Tha, I presagi, Riti: I funerali di Alessandro Magno, Trio,
   Manto per quattro, Kya et al.]
Michiko Hirayama, Maurizio Ben Omar, Federico Mondelci,
   Nuovo Ensemble Italiano, Gruppo Musica Insieme, Aldo Brizzi
INA, CD, INA mémoire vive 247172

Giacinto Scelsi. Music for Wind Instruments and Percussion
Jacques Meertens, Rien De Reede, Thies Roorda, Jan Spronk et al.
Attacca–BABEL, CD, 9479

1996
Giacinto Scelsi. Suite no. 10 ("Ka"), Suite no. 9 ("Ttai")
Markus Hinterhäuser
Col Legno, CD, WWE 1CD 31889

1997
Giacinto Scelsi. The Complete Works for Clarinet
David Smeyers, Susanne Mohr, Ensemble Avance, Zsolt Nagy
cpo, CD, 999 266-2

1998
Giacinto Scelsi: Chamber Works for Flute and Piano
Carin Levine, Peter Veale, Kristi Becker
cpo, CD, 999 340-2

1999

Giacinto Scelsi. Complete Works for Flute and Clarinet
Ebony Duo
Col Legno, CD, WWE 1 CD 20035

Giacinto Scelsi. Kya
Marcus Weiss, Johannes Schmidt, Ensemble Contrechamps,
  with Jürg Wyttenbach
hat[now]ART, CD, hat[now]ART 117

Giacinto Scelsi. Yamaon, Anahit, I presagi, Tre pezzi, Okanagon
Klangforum Wien, Hans Zender et al.
Kairos, CD, 0012032KAI

2000

*Giacinto Scelsi 1. The Piano Works 1: Sonatas no. 2 and no. 4,
  Suite no. 9 ("Ttai")*
Louise Bessette
Mode, CD, mode 92

Giacinto Scelsi. Intégrale de la musique de chambre pour orchestre à cordes
Orchestre Royal de Chambre de Wallonie, with Jean-Paul Dessy
Forlane, CD, Forlane 16800

2001

Giacinto Scelsi. *Intégrale des Œuvres Chorales*
New London Chamber Choir, Percussive Rotterdam, James Wood
Accord, CD, 465 401-2 (reissue of Accord, CD, 206812, 1999)

*Giacinto Scelsi. Streichquartett nr. 4, Elohim, Duo, Anagamin,
  Maknongan, Natura renovatur*
Klangforum Wien, Hans Zender et al.
Kairos, CD (*SmartPac*), 0012162KAI

Giacinto Scelsi 3. Music for High Winds
Carol Robinson, Clara Novakova, Cathy Milliken
Mode, CD, mode 102

Giacinto Scelsi 2. The Orchestral Works 1: Hymnos, Hurqualia, Konx-Om-Pax, Canti del Capricorno
Carnegie Mellon Philharmonic and Choir, Juan Pablo Izquierdo, Pauline Vaillancourt, Douglas Ahlstedt et al.
Mode, CD, mode 95

Viaggio al Centro del Suono
[Pranam II, Marcia rituale, Xnoybis, I, II, III, Quartetto n. 3, Quays, Kya I, II, III]
Ensemble Siddhartha, Nicola Cisternino
Luna Editore, book with CD

2002
Giacinto Scelsi
[Pranam, Anagamin, Quattro pezzi (su una nota sola), Quartetto n. 4, Okanagon, Quartetto n. 2]
Ensemble Oriol Berlin, Ensemble 2E2M, Michiko Hirayama, Luca Pfaff, Antonio Pellegrini et al.
Edition RZ, CD, Ed. RZ 1014

Giacinto Scelsi. Hurqualia, Hymnos, Chukrum
Orchestre de la Radio-Télévision Polonaise de Cracovie, with Jürg Wyttenbach
Accord, CD, 464 257-2 (reissue of Accord, CD, 201112, 1990)

Giacinto Scelsi 5. String Quartets, String Trio, Khoom
Arditti String Quartet
Montaigne, 2 CD, MO 782156 (reissue of *Giacinto Scelsi. Les cinq quatuors à cordes, Trio à cordes, Khoom*, Éditions Salabert, 2 CD, SCD 8904-5, 1990)

Giacinto Scelsi. Trilogia, Ko-Tha
Frances-Marie Uitti
Etcetera, CD, KTC 1136 (reissue of Fore, LP, FORE 80/SIX, 1982)

2003
Giacinto Scelsi. Action Music no. 1, Suite no. 8
Bernhard Wambach
Kairos, CD, 0012312KAI

Giacinto Scelsi. Quattro illustrazioni, Suite no. 8 (Bot-Ba), Cinque incantesimi
Markus Hinterhäuser
Col Legno, CD, WWE 1CD 20068

2004

Scelsi. Œuvres pour Chœur et Orchestre
Jürg Wyttenbach, Orchestre de La Radio-Télévision Polonaise de Cracovie, Chœur de la Philharmonie de Cracovie
Accord, 3 CD, 476 1072 (reissue of *Giacinto Scelsi (1905–1988).*
  Œuvre Intégrale pour Chœur et Orchestre Symphonique, Accord, 3 CD, 201692, 1988–1990)

2005

Incantations. The Art of Song of Giacinto Scelsi
[*Sauh I–IV, Taiagarù, Hô*]
Marianne Schuppe
New Albion, CD, NA 129

Giacinto Scelsi. Suono Rotondo
[Solo Works and Trio Improvisations]
Michael Kiedaisch, Stefano Scodanibbio, Mike Svoboda
WERGO, CD, WER 6672 2

Giacinto Scelsi 4. The Piano Works 2: Suite no. 2, Action Music
Stephen Clarke
Mode, CD, mode 143

2006

Giacinto Scelsi 6. The Orchestral Works 2: La nascita del Verbo,
  Quattro pezzi (su una nota sola), Uaxuctum
Vienna Radio Symphony Orchestra, Concentus Vocalis, Wiener Kammerchor, Peter Rundel, Johannes Kalitzke
Mode, CD, mode 176

Giacinto Scelsi 5. The Piano Works 3: Piano Works in Surround Sound—Aitsi,
  Cinque incantesimi, Quattro Illustrazioni, Sonate no. 3, Suite no. 10 ("Ka"),
  Un adieu
Aki Takahashi
Mode, DVD, CD, mode 159

Giacinto Scelsi: Natura renovatur
Frances-Marie Uitti, Münchener Kammerorchester, Christoph Poppen
ECM New Series, CD, ECM 1963, ECM New Seires 3106

2007
Giacinto Scelsi 7. The Works for Double Bass: Dharana, Et maintenant c'est à vous de jouer, Ko-Tha, Kshara, Maknongan, Mantram, Nuits, Okanagon
Robert Black et al.
Mode, mode 188, CD, 2007, United States

Giacinto Scelsi. Collection vol.1
[Mahnongan, Quartetto n. 2, Riti: I funerali d'Achille, Quattro illustrazioni sulle metamorfosi di Vishnu, Riti: I funerali di Carlo Magno]
Musicateatroensemble, Enrico Cocco, Quartetto D'Archi di Torino, Roberto Fabbriciani, Francesco Dillon, Fulvia Ricevuto, Fabrizio Ottaviucci et al.
Stradivarius, CD, STR 33801

Giacinto Scelsi. Collection vol. 2
[Pranam II, To the Master, Wo Ma, Rotativa, Trio, Preghiera per un'ombra, Chukrum]
Nicholas Isherwood, Carlo Teodoro, Véronique Fèvre et al.
Stradivarius, CD, STR 33802

Gacinto Scelsi. Canti del Capricorno
Michiko Hirayama et al.
Wergo, CD, WER 6686 2 (reissue of WERGO CD/LP, WER 60127-50, 1988)

Giacinto Scelsi. Trilogia, I tre stadi dell'uomo
Arne Deforce
æon, CD, AECD 0748

2008
Giacinto Scelsi. Musica Viva 17: Chukrum, Quattro pezzi, Natura renovatur, Hymnos
Symphonieorchester des Bayerischen Rundfunks, Hans Zender, Peter Rundel et al.
Neos, CD, NEOS 10722

Giacinto Scelsi. Collection vol. 4
[*12 preludi, Variazioni e fuga, Capriccio, Poemi, Rotativa*]
Donna Amato
Stradivarius, CD, STR 33804

2009
Giacinto Scelsi. Collection vol. 3
[*Aiôn, Hymnos, Quattro pezzi per orchestra, Ballata*]
Orchestra Sinfonica Nazionale della RAI, Ensemble di Percussioni Naqqara, Tito Ceccherini, Francesco Dillon et al.
Stradivarius, CD, STR 33803

Giacinto Scelsi. Preludi, serie I–IV
Alessandra Ammara
ARTS, CD, Arts Music 47721-8

2010
Giacinto Scelsi 8. The Piano Works 4. Hispania, Suite no. 5 ("Il Circo"), Suite no. 6 ("I capricci di Ty")
Stephen Clarke
Mode, CD, mode 227

Giacinto Scelsi. Tre canti popolari, Due componimenti impetuosi
Johan Bossers et al.
Sub Rosa, 2 CD, SR302 (reissue of Sub Rosa, CD, SR63, 1995)

2011
Giacinto Scelsi 9. The Viola Works
[*Manto, Coelocanth, Elegia per Ty, Three Studies, Xnoybis*]
Vincent Royer, Séverine Ballon et al.
Mode, CD, mode 231

2013
Giacinto Scelsi. Collection vol. 5
[*Quartetto per archi n. 1, Trio per archi, Quartetto per archi n. 2, Khoom, Quartetto per archi nn. 3, 4, 5*]
Arditti String Quartet et al.
Stradivarius, 2 CD, STR 33805

Giacinto Scelsi 10. The Violin Works
Weiping Lin
Mode, CD, mode 256

Giacinto Scelsi. Chamber Music
[with *To The Master* (1974); two improvisations with Victoria Parr, for violoncello and piano]
Ensemble Avantgarde
MDG, CD, MDG 613 1802-2

2014
Giacinto Scelsi, Collection vol. 6
[*Maknongan, Pwyll, Hyxos, Quays, Tetraktys, Maknongan*]
Robeeto Fabbriciani, and Jonathan Faralli
Stradivarius, CD, STR 33806

RITO. Giacinto Scelsi
[*Pranam I, Pranam II, Khoom, Riti: I funerali Di Alessandro Magno, Okanagon*]
Ensemble Phoenix Basel, with Marianne Schuppe
Telos Music, CD, TLS 191

2015
Giacinto Scelsi. Suite 9 & 10 per pianoforte
[Suite n. 9 ("Ttai"), Suite n. 10 ("Ka")]
Sabine Liebner
WERGO, CD, WER 6794 2

2016
Giacinto Scelsi. Complete Flute Music
[Hyxos, Suite for flute and clarinet, Quays, Rucke Di Guck, Ko-Lho, Tetratkys, Krishna e Rada]
Claudia Giottoli, with Natalia Benedetti et al.
Brilliant Classics, CD, 95039

2017
Giacinto Scelsi. Collection vol. 7
[Suite n. 6 ("I capricci di Ty"), Divertimento n. 1, L'Âme Ailée / L'Âme Ouverte, Xnoybis]
Anna D'Errico, with Marco Fusi
Stradivarius, CD, STR 33807

Giacinto Scelsi. Collection vol. 8
[*Chemin du Cœur, Dialogo, Sonata, Trio*]
Alessandro Stella, Markus Däunert, Giovanni Gnocchi
Stradivarius, CD, STR 33808

Scelsi. Music for Cello Solo
[*Triphon, Dithome, Ygghur, Voyages*]
Marco Simonacci
Brilliant Classics, CD, 95355

Giacinto Scelsi. Opere per pianoforte
[*Quattro illustrazioni per piano solo, Suite n. 9 ("Ttai")*]
Rossella Spinosa
Tactus, CD, TC 901901

2020
Giacinto Scelsi. String Trio
London Contemporary Orchestra, with Max Ruisi, Robert Ames, Galya Bisengalieva
SA Recordings, LP, SA021

Giacinto Scelsi, *Suite 8 & 11 per pianoforte*
Sabine Liebner
WERGO, CD, WER 73282

Giacinto Scelsi. Suite no. 9, Quattro illustrazioni, Un adieu
Shira Legmann
Elsewhere, CD, elsewhere 013

2021
Giacinto Scelsi. Works For Violin And For Viola
Marco Fusi
Kairos, CD, 0015063KAI

***

Collections

[Date unknown]
Jean-Pierre Caens, and Philippe Bouveret, *Musiques du vingtième siècle: Duo de saxophones*
Music by Christian Lauba, Giacinto Scelsi (*Tre pezzi pour saxophone soprano seul*), Paul Hindemith, François-Bernard Mâche
Philippe Viard Editeur, Editions Chrismiphil, CD, PVE 923521-3

1972
New Music for String Quartet
Music by Pierre Boulez, Giacinto Scelsi (B1: *Quartetto d'archi no. 4, Quartetto di Nuova Musica*), Earle Brown
Quatuor Parrenin, Das Hamann Quartett, Quartetto di Nuova Musica, New York String Quartet
Mainstream Records, LP, 1972, MS/5009

1974
Nuove Forme Sonore
Music by Giancarlo Schiaffini, Frances-Marie Uitti, Mauro Bortolotti, Michele Iannaccone, Giacinto Scelsi (B2: *HO II, V*), Bruno Maderna, John Cage
Frances-Marie Uitti, Marcello Rosa, Massimo Rocci et al.
Curci, LP, SPL 915

Paul Zukofsky, *Giacinto Scelsi, Iannes Xanakis, Philip Glass*
Music by Giacinto Scelsi (*Anahit*), Iannes Xenakis, Philip Glass
CP2 Recordings, LP, CP2/6

1984
Daniel Kientzy, *Instrumenta 3. Saxophone(s) Solo*
Music by Luciano Berio, François Rossé, Paul Méfano, Giacinto Scelsi (B2: *Tre pezzi*), Betsy Jolas, Daniel Kientzy
Poly-Art Records, LP, PAR 5303

Musiques trans-alpines (vol. 1)
Music by Giacinto Scelsi (*Natura renovatur*), Alessandro Sbordoni, Robert Pascal, Alain Savouret
Griffith Rose

Ensemble Alternance, Luca Pfaff, Pascal Bonnier, Maria Licata,
   Claire-Marie Mille, Kyoko Okumura, Marie Helene Huguel,
   Gérard Chouquer, Centre Polyphonique de Franche-Comte
Adda, LP, CCS 590013

1986
9° Festival internazionale di musica contemporanea. La lente sui margini
Music by Costin Miereanu, Daniel Tosi, Gacinto Scelsi (B1: *Okanagon*,
   Ensemble Antidogma, Daniel Tosi et al.; B3: *Rotative*, Fabio Luz,
   Marinella Tarenghi), Enrico Correggia, James Dillon, Niccolò Castiglioni
   Aurel Stroe, Bernard Cavanna, Giuseppe Giuliano
Icons Antidogma Records, 2 LP, AM-I 861-862

Joëlle Léandre, David Thomas, and The Wooden Birds, *April U Beogradu*
Music by Jakob Druckman, Joëlle Léandre, Betsy Jolas, Steve Lacy,
   Giacinto Scelsi (A6: *C'est bien la nuit*, Joëlle Léandre), John Cage,
   David Thomas, and the Wooden Birds
Nikad Robom, Cassette, 003

Rencontre & Création
Music by Giacinto Scelsi (A1: *Natura renovatur pour 11 cordes*, Ensemble
   Alternance, with Luca Pfaff), Alessandro Sbordoni, Griffith Rose,
   Alain Savouret
Ensemble Alternance, Luca Pfaff, Quatuor Arcadie, Pascale Bonnier,
   Ensemble Vocal Amateur, Marie Helene Huguel, Gerard Chouquer
Horizon Vert, LP, HV 8602

1987
10° Festival internazionale di musica contemporanea
Music by Costin Miereanu, Enrico Correggia, Giacinto Scelsi (B1: *I presagi*,
   Nantes Percussion, Will Humburg et al.), Paul Méfano, Enrique X. Macias,
   Ada Gentile, Philippe Hersant, Gilbert Ami, Mihai Mitrea Celarianu,
   Giorgio Tedde
Nantes Percussion, Will Humburg, Ensemble 2E2M et al.
Icons Antidogma Records, 2 LP, Am-I 871-872

1988

11° Festival Internazionale di Musica Contemporanea
Music by Giacinto Scelsi (*Ko-Tha*), Costin Miereanu, Enrico Correggia, Enrique X. Macias
Dora Filippone et al.
Adda, CD, 581157

Daniel Kientzy, *Saxophone(s) et dispositif électroacoustique*
Music by Luciano Berio, Karlheinz Stockhausen, Giacinto Scelsi (*Tre pezzi*), Aurel Stroe, François-Bernard Mâche, Bernard Cavana, Horacio Vaggione
ADDA, CD, 581047

New Music Series (vol. 2)
Music by Luciano Berio, Giacinto Scelsi (*Five Incantations*, Kathleen Supove), Roger Reynolds, Nancy Barney, Brian Ferneyhough, Robert Cogan
Piere-Yves Artaud, Joan Heller, Gordon Stout, Kathleen Supove, Arthur Haas, Dorothy Bastian, Emily Laurance
Neuma, CD, Neuma 45072

Pierre-André Valade, *Flûte*
Music by Steve Reich, Giacinto Scelsi (*Ko-Lho*), Philippe Durville, York Höller, Philippe Hurel, Jean-Marc Singier, Philippe Manoury, Klaus Huber, Françoise Rossé
Pierre-André Valade, Rémi Lerner, Isabelle Veyrier, Ichirô Nodaïra
Adda, CD, 581075

1989

Joëlle Léandre, *Contrebasse et voix / Double Bass and Voice*
Music by Betsy Jolas, Giacinto Scelsi (*C'est bien la nuit, Le réveil profond, Maknongan*), John Cage, Jacob Durckman, Joëlle Léandre, Sylvano Bussotti, Sharon Kanach
Adda, CD, 581043

Hendrik Niehoff, *Collection*
Music by Arnold Schönberg, Benjamin Britten, John Cage, Huub ten Hacken, Mauricio Kagel, Zoltán Kodaly, Darius Milhaud, Erik Satie, Giacinto Scelsi (*Suite no. 10 "Ka"* [two movements only]), Igor Stravinsky
With Huub ten Hacken
Hendrik Niehoff, CD, HN 890524

Le trombone contemporain
Music by Henri Dutilleux, René Leibowitz, Giacinto Scelsi (*Tre pezzi*),
   Luciano Berio, Edison Denisov, Gerald Barry Anderson, Iannis Xenakis,
   Pascal Dusapin
Benny Sluchin, and Pierre-Laurent Aimard
ADDA, 581087, CD, 1989

1990
Neuma New Music Series (vol. 1)
Music by Iannis Xenakis, Jean-Claude Risset, Giacinto Scelsi (*Tre pezzi*),
   Shirish Korde
Benny Sluchin, Mel Culbertson et al.
Neuma, CD, Neuma 45071

Pauline Vaillancourt, *Récitations; Canti del Capricorno*
Music by Georges Aperghis, and Giacinto Scelsi (*Canti del Capricorno*)
SNE, CD, SNE 571

1991
Werner Bärtschi, *Klang Klavier*
Music by John Cage, Giacinto Scelsi (*Aitsi*), Thomas Kessler, Karlheinz
   Stockhausen, Henry Cowell, Steve Ingham
RecRec Music, CD, ReCDec 04 (reissue of RecRec Music, LP, RecRec 04,
   1984)

Pierre Bousseau, *Au grand orgue de la Cathédrale Notre-Dame du Harve*
Music by Györgi Ligeti, Claude Vivier, Bernard Cavanna, Giacinto Scelsi
   (*In nomine lucis*), Jaques Lenot, Jeannine Richer, Arvo Pärt
Adda, CD, ADDA 581240

Hilde Torgersen - Kenneth Karlsson
Music by Giacinto Scelsi (*Hô*), Bjorn Howard Kruse, Asbjorn Schaathun,
   James Dillon, Rolf Wallin
Hilde Torgersen, Kenneth Karlsson, and The Cikada Ensemble
Albedo, CD, ALBCD 003

1992
Music of Our Century (Musik Unserer Zeit)
Music by Györgi Ligeti, Paul Hindemith, Karlheinz Stockausen, John Cage,
   Cathy Barberian, Giacinto Scelsi (*Canti del Capricorno*), Hans Werner
   Henze, Krzysztof Penderecki, Meredith Monk, Harald Weiss, Charles Ives
Percussion Today, Lejaren Hiller
WERGO, CD, WER 60200-50

1993
Disque catalogue, Sampler
Music by J. S. Bach, Henry Purcell, Alexis de Castillon, Henri Duparc,
   Joseph Haydn, Gabriel Fauré, Wolfgang Amadeus Mozart, Giacinto Scelsi
   (*Riti: I funerali di Alessandro Magno*), Claude Debussy, Johannes Brahms
INA, CD, INA 282011

Reinhold Friedrich
Music by Bernd Alois Zimmermann, Luciano Berio, Wolfgang Rihm,
   Giacinto Scelsi (*Vier Stücke* [für trompete solo]), Wilhelm Killmayer
Reinhold Friedrich, Radio Sinfonie Orchester Frankfurt, Dimitrij Kitajenko
Capriccio, CD, Capriccio 10482

Haydée Schvartz, *New Piano Works from Europe and the Americas*
Music by Arvo Pärt, John Cage, Giacinto Scelsi (*Quattro illustrazioni*),
   Mauricio Kagel, Luciano Berio, Robert Schumann, Gerardo Gandini,
   Gabriel Valverde
Mode, CD, mode 31

1994
Maurizio Barbetti
Music by Aldo Brizzi, Franco Donatoni, Morton Feldman, Luca Francesconi,
   Toshio Hosokawa, Ennio Morricone, Robert H. P. Platz, Giacinto Scelsi
   (*Manto I*), Salvatore Sciarrino, Gilles Silvestrini
Music Worz, CD, PHM 9409826 B

Claude Delangle, *The Solitary Saxophone*
Music by Karlheinz Stockhausen, Luciano Berio, Giacinto Scelsi
(*Maknongan, Ixor, Tre pezzi*), Betsy Jolas, Tōru Takemitsu
BIS, CD, BIS-CD-640

James Fulkerson, *Ladder of Escape 8*
Music by James Fulkerson, Giacinto Scelsi (*Maknongan*), Earle Brown,
 Alfred del Monaco, John Cage, Louis Andriessen
Attacca, CD, BABEL 9477

Klaus Huber, *Giacinto Scelsi*
Music by Klaus Huber, Giacinto Scelsi (*I presagi*, Cologne Ensemble,
 Robert Platz)
Thorofon, CD, CTH 2015

Werner Bartschi, *Mozart, Scelsi, Pärt, Bärtschi, Busoni*
Music by Wolfgang Amadeus Mozart, Giacinto Scelsi (*Vier Illustrationen zu
 den Verwandlungen Vishnus*), Arvo Pärt, Ferruccio Busoni, Werner Bärtschi
ECM Records, ECM New Series, ECM 1377, 839 659-2, 1994, Germany

Voxnova: *Scelsi, Byzantium, The Alchemists*
Music by various artists (Giacinto Scelsi, *Three Songs of Capricorn*, CKCKC
 I–II, *Le grand sanctuaire I–II*, *Three Latin Players*)
Pascal Sausy, Nicholas Isherwood, Julian Pike, Pascal Sausy
hat ART, CD, hat ART CD 6148

1995
25 Jaar Nieuwe Muziek in Zeeland
Music by Willem Breuker, Ivan Wyschnegradsky, Luca Francesconi,
 Diamanda Galas, Morton Gould, Leo Cuypers, Iannes Xenakis,
 Floris van Manen, Giacinto Scelsi (*Le fleuve magique*,
 Frances-Marie Uitti), Morton Feldman
BV Haast Records, CD, 9501

Corrado Canonici: *Contrabass*
Music by Dinu Ghezzo, Luciano Berio, Luca Macchi, Suzanne Giraud,
 Daniel Kessner, Giacinto Scelsi (*Maknongan*), John Cage, Ronald Mazurek
Capstone, CD, CPS-8628

Arditti String Quartet, *From Italy. Berio, Bussotti, Castiglioni, Donatoni,
 Maderna, Melchiorre, Scelsi, Sciarrino, Scodanibbio, Stroppa*
Music by Franco Donatoni, Stefano Scodanibbio, Sylvano Bussotti,
 Alessandro Melchiorre, Niccolò Castiglioni, Giacinto Scelsi (*String Quartet
 no. 4*), Bruno Maderna, Luciano Berio, Salvatore Sciarrino, Marco Stroppa
Disques Montaigne, CD, Montaigne 782042

Klangforum Wien, *Live at Konzerthaus*
Music by Giacinto Scelsi (*I presagi*), Hans Zender, Wolfram Schurig,
　Andreas Lindenbaum, Donna Wagner Molinari, Michael Gross,
　Uli Fussenegger, Helmut Lachenman, Arnold Schönberg, Beat Furrer,
　Mayako Kubo
Durian, 2 CD, Durian 097 / 098-2

Livia Mazzanti, *Visioni del Novecento. Schoenberg, Messiaen, Hindemith, Scelsi*
Music by Arnold Schönberg, Olivier Messiaen, Paul Hindemith,
　Giacinto Scelsi (*In nomine lucis*)
Fonè, CD, Fonè 9203

Christoph Maria Moosmann, *Annum per Annum*
Music by Arvo Pärt, John Cage, Giacinto Scelsi (*In nomine lucis*)
New Albion, CD, NA 074 CD

Ensemble Nunc
Music by Isang Yun, Detlev Glanert, Cord Meijering, Giacinto Scelsi
　(*Ko-Tha*), Gerhard Müller-Hornbach, Rolf Riehm, Klaus Hinrich Stahmer
Signum, CD, SIG X61-00

Paul Zukofsky, *Brant, Scelsi, Wolpe, Xenakis, Cage, Glass, Feldman*
Music by Henry Brant, Giacinto Scelsi (*Anahit*), Stefan Wolpe,
　Iannes Xenakis, John Cage, Philip Glass, Morton Feldman
CP2 Recordings, CD, CP2/108

1996
Darmstadt 1946–1996. 50 Years of New Music
Music by various artists (Giacinto Scelsi, CD 2: *Ko-Tha, version for double
　bass*, Fernando Grillo; CD 3: *Un adieu*, Marianne Schroeder)
Col Legno, 4 CD, WWE 4CD 31893

Petr Matuszek, *Na Prahu Světla*
Music by Petr Pokorný, Martin Smolka, Giacinto Scelsi (*Ave Maria,
　Pater noster, Alleluja*), Michal Macourek, Miloslav Kabeláč
Happy Music Production, CD, HMP 0012 P

Nouvelles Musiques de Chambre
Music by Henri Pousseur, Bernard Foccroulle, Michel Fourgon,
    Frederic D'Haene, Edison Denisov, Giacinto Scelsi (*Anahit* for violin and
    18 instruments)
Liège New Music Ensemble, Jean-Pierre Peuvion
Cypres, CD, CYP4601

1997
Eduard Brunner, *Dal niente*
Music by Lachenmann, Karlheinz Stockhausen, Igor Stravinsky,
    Pierre Boulez, Giacinto Scelsi (*Preghiera per un'ombra*), Isang Yun
ECM New Series, CD, ECM New Series 1599, 453 257-2

Iris Gerber, *Strutture per pianoforte*
Music by Franco Evangelisti, Luigi Nono, Daniel Ritter, Geneviève Calame,
    Giacinto Scelsi (*Aïtsi, Quattro illustrazioni*)
Edition Bianchi-Neri, CD [code unknown]

Hans Zender, *Edition no. 13: Scelsi / Zender*
Music by Giacinto Scelsi (*Quattro pezzi per orchestra; Pranam*)
Rundfunk-Sinfonieorchester Saarbrücken
cpo, CD, 999 485-2

1998
Keiko Hatanaka, *A New Asian Voice* (vol. 1)
Music by Scelsi (*Taiagarù*), Toshio Hosokowa, Toshi Ichiyanagi,
    John Cage, Tan Dun, Luciano BerioKeiko Hatanaka et al.
Ta Ra Ga, CD, TRG-002

Keiko Hatanaka, *Philomēla*
Music by Giacinto Scelsi (*Hô*), Keiko Hatanaka
Ta Ra Ga, CD, TRG-001

Björn Lanke, and Siri Toriesen, *The Contemporary Double Bass* (vol. 1)
Music by Antonio Bibalo, Giacinto Scelsi (*C'est bien la nuit*), Luciano Berio,
    Peter Huber, Åsmund Feidje
Simax Classic, CD, PSC 1136

1999
Lutz Mandler, *Atemwege: Breath Paths*
Music by Otto Ketting, Stan Friedman, Ali N. Askin, Robert Erickson,
   Kühnl, Giacinto Scelsi (*Quattro pezzi*), Nikolaus Heyduck,
   Tōru Takemitsu, David Sampson
Cadenza, CD, CAD 800 876

Stefano Cogolo, *Fludance*
Stefano Cogolo, Terje Bjorklund, Giacinto Scelsi (*Quays*),
   Domenico Guaccero, Pierre-Octave Ferroud, Antonio Scarlato,
   Claude Debussy, Astor Piazzolla, Jacques Ibert, Alessandro Murzi,
   Henri Tomasi, Alberto Giraldi
DMCD, CD, DMCD 9901

Neue Vocalsolisten Stuttgart, *Porträt*
Music by Josquin des Préz, Dieter Schnebel, Sylvano Bussotti,
   Pascal Dusapin, Olga Neuwirth, Brian Ferneyhough, Younghi Pagh-Paan,
   Iannis Xenakis, Giacinto Scelsi (CD 2: *Tre canti sacri*)
Neue Vocalsolisten Stuttgart, with Manfred Schreier
Col Legno, CD, WWE 2 CD 20030

2000
David Kappy, *Gone*
Music by David Kappy, Giacinto Scelsi (*Quattro pezzi*), Daniel Harris
David Kappy, with Daniel Harris
Andrew Will Recording, CD [code unknown]

Kenneth Karlsson, *Sofferte onde serene. Music by Nono, Berio, Scelsi*
Music by Luigi Nono, Luciano Berio, Giacinto Scelsi (*Suite no. 10 "Ka"*)
Albedo, CD, ALBCD 015 (also Norway Music, CD, NMP 015)

Daniele Lombardi, *Futurismusic. Piano Anthology 1*
Music by Franco Casavola, Alberto Savino, Giacinto Scelsi (*Rotativa*),
   Vergilio Mortari, Aldo Giuntini, Chesimò [Mario Monachesi],
   Daniele Napoletano, Gian Francesco Malipiero, Germaine Albert Birot,
   Igor Stravinsky, Alfredo Casella
Col Legno, CD, WWE 1CD 20076

Mats Möller, *Solo per Flauto*
Music by various artists (Giacinto Scelsi, CD 1: *Pwyll*)
SFZ Records, 2 CD, SFZ 2001

Anette Maria Slaatto, *The Secret Melody*
Music by Nørgård, Dinescu, Giacinto Scelsi (*Coelacanth*), Frounberg
Ambitus, CD, Ambitus 96823

Mike Svoboda, *Power and Poetry*
Music by Brio, Morton Feldman, Giacinto Scelsi (*Tre pezzi*), Iannes Xenakis,
d'c records, CD, dc12

Elisabeth Klein, *The Modern Italian Piano*
Music by Giacinto Scelsi (*Sonata no. 3*), Luciano Berio, Luigi Dallapiccola,
    Sylvano Bussotti, Franco Evangelisti
Classico, CD, CLASSCD259

Unclassical O, I
Music by Marcel Duchamp, Renaud De Putter, Luigi Dallapiccola,
    Brett Dean, Paolo Chagas, Claude Debussy, Luigi Russolo,
    Henri Pousseur, Giacinto Scelsi (*Duo for Violin and Cello*, part 1),
    Georg-Alexander Van Dam et al.
Sub Rosa, CD, SR138

2001
Entmilitarisierte Zonen Märsche
Music by Kurt Weill, Johann Strauss, Mauricio Kagel, H. K. Gruber,
    Wolfgang Rihm, Ludwig van Beethoven, Giacinto Scelsi (*Riti "Ritual
    March,"* version for Achilles), Richard Wagner, Emmanuel Chabrier,
    Sergei Prokofiev, Abe Holzmann, Scott Joplin
Hr Brass, and Lutz Kohler
Capriccio, CD, 10839

Roberto Fabbriciani, Massimiliano Damerini, Jonathan Faralli, *Hyxos*
Music by Giacinto Scelsi (*Hyxos*), Nicola Sani, Claudio Vaira,
    Mauricio Sotelo, Daniele Lombardi, John Cage, Franco Donatoni
Agorà Musica, CD, AG. 275

Nuits
Music by Toshio Hosokawa, Giacinto Scelsi (*Tre canti sacri per 8 voci miste, TKRDG*), Arnold Schönberg, René Leibowitz, Anton Webern, Cornelius Schwehr, Iannes Xenakis, György Ligeti
Schola Heidelberg ensemble, with Walter Nussbaum
BIS, CD, BIS-CD-1090

Hilde Torgersen, *Voice Stories*
Music by Alejandro Viñao, Giacinto Scelsi (*Hô, Taiagaru*), Luigi Nono
Albedo, CD, ALBCD 012

2002
Apollo and Marsyas: Het Apollohuis 1980–1997.
An Anthology of New Music Concepts
Music by various artists (Giacinto Scelsi, CD 2: *Ka*, Reinier Van Houdt)
Het Apollohuis/Apollo Records 2 CD 2002, ACD 090217

Chorklang im 20. Jahrhundert
Music by Florent Schmitt, Heitor Villa-Lobos, Luigi Dallapiccola, György Ligeti, Giacinto Scelsi (*Tre canti sacri*), Ildebrando Pizzetti
Wiener Konzertchor, Gottfried Rabl
ORF, CD, ORF 95

Garth Knox, *Spectral Viola*
Music by Gerard Grisey, Georg Friedrich Haas, Tristan Murail, Giacinto Scelsi (*Manto I, II*), Horatiu Radulescu
Edition Zeitklang, CD, EZ 10012

Plot in Fiction
Music by Enrique Correggia, Luca Francesconi, Giacinto Scelsi (*Kya*), Ada Gentile, Dario Maggi
Firebird Ensemble, Webb Barrie
Metier, CD, Metier 92018

Ponder Nothing
Music by Steve Reich, Giacinto Scelsi (*Tre pezzi per saxophone*, Susan Fancher), Ben Johnston, Mark Engebretson, Wolfram Wagner, Alexander Wagendristel
Innova records, CD, Innova records 546

Trio Kya with Febian Reza Pane
Music by Ana-Maria Avram, Giacinto Scelsi (*Canti del Capricorno,
    Tre pezzi*), John Cage, Gustavo Aguilar, Iancu Dumitrescu, Robert Reigle,
    Keiko Hatanaka, Reza Pane
Gustavo Aguilar, Febian Reza Pane, Robert Reigle, Keiko Hatanaka
Ta Ra Ga, CD-r, TRG-LO-006

2003

Leon Michener, *Imaginary Landscapes*
Music by John Cage, Charles Ives, Giacinto Scelsi (*Aitsi*), Iannes Xenakis,
Future Music Records, CD, FMR 95 C 0602

2004

20 Jahre Inventionen II
Music by Hildegard Westerkamp, Salvatore Sciarrino, John Cage,
    Sainkho Namtchylak, Joe Jones, Giacinto Scelsi (*Canti del Capricorno
    no. 1, no. 4*, Michiko Hirayama), Masanori Fujita, John Driscoll
Edition RZ CD 2004, Ed. RZ 4004

Friedemann Herz, *Zeit*
Music by Wolfgang Rihm, Peter Ruzicka, Morton Feldman,
    Giacinto Scelsi (*In nomine lucis*), Hans Joachim Hespos
aulos, CD, AUL 66097 (reissue of Koch Schwa, CD,
    Koch International 3-1339, 1993)

Portrait, CD Mondrian Ensemble
Music by Iannes Xenakis, Michel Roth, Giacinto Scelsi (*Trio à cordes*)
Mondrian Ensemble
Musique Suisses/Grammont Portrait/Schweizer Radio DRS2, CD,
    CTS-M 88

Dan Styffe, *Revisited*
Music by Astor Piazzolla, John Persen, Giacinto Scelsi (*Maknongan*),
    Teppo Hauta-Aho, Gisle Kverndokk, Iannes Xenakis, Paul Ramsier
Simax Classic, CD, PSC 1252

2005
Marco Blaauw, *Blaauw*
Music by Gerald Barry, Richard Ayres, Rebecca Saunders, Giacinto Scelsi
 (*Quattro pezzi*), Egmont Swaan, Isabel Mundry, Tōru Takemitsu,
 György Kurtag, Karlheinz Stockhausen
BV Haast Records, CD, CD 0805

Chamber
Music by Jullian Carrillo, Lou Harrison, Giacinto Scelsi (*Ko-Lho*,
 Michiyo Suzuki, Andrew Bolotowsky), Iannes Xenakis, Charles Ives,
 Harry Partch
American Festival of Microtonal Music Ensemble, and Johnny Reinhard
Pitch, CD, 200203

Chanticleer, *Sound in Spirit*
Music by Jan Gilbert, Nectarie Vlahul, Joseph Jennings,
 Carlos Rafael Rivera, Tomas Luis de Victoria, Jackson Hill,
 Giacinto Scelsi (*Gloria in excelsis Deo*, from *Tre canti sacri*),
 Sarah Hopkins, Patricia Van Ness Warner Classics, CD, 11292 12

Jessika Kuhn, *Giacinto Scelsi*
Music by Giacinto Scelsi (*Trilogia*), Ali-Sade
Thorofon, CD, CTH 2480

Sabina Meyer, *Cruelly Coy*
Music by Giacinto Scelsi (*Hô I, Hô II, Taiagarù*), Luciano Berio, John Cage,
 Erik Satie, Hanns Eisler
Lazy Melodies, CD, LM 1001

Arturo Tallini, *BLU*
Music by Nuccio D'Angelo, Goffredo Petrassi, Mario Dall'Ongaro,
 Giacinto Scelsi (*Ko-Tha, Tre danze di Shiva*), Dimitri Nicolau,
 Gianvincenzo Cresta, Benjamin Britten
Tempi Moderni Edizioni CD 2005, TM 003

La voce contemporanea in Italia (vol. 1)
Music by Azio Corghi, Luigi Dallapiccola, Domenico Guaccero,
 Goffredo Petrassi, Ricardo Piacentini, Giacinto Scelsi (*Tre canti di primavera*)
Duo Alterno, Tiziana Scandaletti, Riccardo Piacentini
Stradivarius, CD, STR 33708

2006
Salvatore Cicero Violinista
Music by various artists (Giacinto Scelsi, CD 1: *Xnoybis*)
In *Salvatore Cicero Violinista*. Edited by Girolamo Garofalo. Palermo: Archivio Sonoro Siciliano

2007
Sonic Rebellion: Alternative Classical Collection
Music by Philip Glass, Krzysztof Penderecki, Conlon Nancarrow, John Cage, Hans Werner Henze, Giacinto Scelsi (*Quattro pezzi per orchestra* I) et al.
Rundfunk-Sinfonieorchester Saarbrücken, Bournemouth Symphony Orchestra
Naxos, CD, 8.570760

2008
Mark Cauvin, *Transfiguration*
Music by Giacinto Scelsi (*Ko-Tha I, II, III*), László Dubrovay, Fernando Grillo, Julien-François Zbinder, Luciano Berio, Iannes Xenakis
2 CD, with the partnership of the Australian Council of the Arts
[code unknown]

Hommage a Scelsi
Music by Giacinto Scelsi (*Sonate pour violin et piano*, Divertimento no. 4, Duo, *Xnoybis*), Bruno Montanari, Diego Tosi, Timothé Tosi, Jay Gottlieb
Disques du Solstice, CD, SOCD 242

Simone Mancuso, *La parola al legno*
Music by Salvatore Sciarrino, John Cage, Giacinto Scelsi (*Maknongan*)
Stradivarius, CD, STR 33863

Murcof, *FACT Mix 10*
Music by Francesco Tristano, Valentin Silvestrov, Giacinto Scelsi (*Konx-Om-Pax*), Johann Johannsson, Arvo Pärt, Pawel Szymanski
FACT Magazine, MP3, FACT 10

Musica Viva Festival 2008
Music by various artistis (Giacinto Scelsi, *Uaxuctum*, Chor und Symphonieorchester des Bayerischen Rundfunks, Emilio Pomárico)
NEOS SACD, 6 CD, NEOS SACD 10926/3

Spire Live, *Fundamentalis*
Music by Philip Jeck, Charles Matthews, Giacinto Scelsi (*In nomine lucis*),
   Marcus Davidson, B. J. Nilsen, Christian Fennesz
Autofact Records/Touch, 2 LP, FACT12/Tone 28

2009
*Der unwiderstehliche Klang der Neuen Musik - The Irresistible Sound of
   Contemporary Music: Audio-Auszüge/-extracts/-extraits/-recortes*
Music by various artists (Giacinto Scelsi, *Anahit*)
Kairos, CD [code unknown]

Lori Freedman, *Bridge*
Music by Lori Freedman, Michel Galante, Pascal Dusapin, Giacinto Scelsi
   (*Maknongan*), Franco Donatoni, Georges Aperghis, Monique Jean
Collection QB, CD, CQB 0909

Duo Hyxos
Music by Korelis, Jean-Jacques Di Tucci, Roger Lersy, François Rossé,
   Alain Féron, Giacinto Scelsi (*Hyxos*), Yoshihisa Taira, Jean-Yves Naviner
   Henri Tournier, Michel Gastaud
Timpani, CD, 1C1032

L'incantesimo dei tanti mondi
Music by Giacinto Scelsi (*Quartetto per archi no. 3*), Mario Berlinguer,
   Roberto Fabbriciani, Adel Karanov, Francesco Lotoro, Orozco Hurtado,
   Nicola Sani
In Ornella Rota, *L'incantesimo dei tanti mondi: Conversazioni con Vincenzo
   Parma*. Rome: Suono Musica Suono Records, CD, SR006

Turning Point Ensemble, *Liquid*
Music by John Korsrud, Yannick Plamondon, Francois Houle,
   Giacinto Scelsi (*Kya*, Françoise Houle)
ATMA Classique, CD, ACD22394

2010
Irmela Nolte, *Flöte Avantgarde*
Music by Cristóbal Hallfter, Giacinto Scelsi (*Pwyll*), Isang Yun,
   George Benjamin, Édison Denisov, Jan Jirásek, Henri Pousseur,
   Goffredo Petrassi Irmela Nolte
Cavalli Record, CD, CCD 1001

Nicola Baroni, *Violoncello italiani XXI sec.*
Music by Alberto Caprioli, Sylvano Bussotti, Massimilliano Massieri, Heinrich Unterhofer, Giacinto Scelsi (*Triphon*), Nicola Cisternino, Claudio Scannavini, Paolo Castaldi, Andrea Costantini
La Bottega Discantica, CD, Discantica 211

Frank Reinecke, *Music for Double Bass*
Music by Giacinto Scelsi (*C'est bien la nuit, Le réveil profond*), Isang Yun, Iannes Xenakis, Hans Manfred Stahnke, Hans Werner Henze, Bent Lorentzen, Frank Reinecke
NEOS, CD, NEOS 11018

Shutter Island (Music from the Motion Picture)
Music by various artists (Giacinto Scelsi, CD 1: *Uaxuctum*)
Rhino Records, 2 CD, R2 522120 (US) - 812279831-9 (Europe)

Snapshots: Developments of Contemporary Classical Music
Music by various artists (Giacinto Scelsi, CD 6: *Piano Sonata no. 3*)
Documents, 10 CD, 233088

Berg. Music of Tribute (vol. 6)
Music by Alban Berg, Giacinto Scelsi (*Poemi no. 4, Passage du poete*, Ieva Jokubaviciute), Franghiz Ali-Zadeh, Ross Lee Finney, Jacob Gilboa, Hans Erich Apostel
Labor Records, CD, LAB 7086

2011
Earle Brown Contemporary Sound Series (vol. 4)
Music by various artists (Giacinto Scelsi, CD 1: *Quartetto d'archi no. 4*)
WERGO 3 CD 2011, WER 6937 2 (reissue of Mainstream Records LP 1972, MS/5009 [CD 1])

Ital. LWE Podcast 97 (vol. 3)
Music by various artists (Giacinto Scelsi, *Streichquartett Nr. 4*)
Little White Earbuds MP3 (320kbps) 2011, LWE097

The Roots Of Drone
Music by various artists (Giacinto Scelsi, CD 2: *Trio for strings*)
Chrome Dreams 2 CD 2011, CDCD5078

Olivier Capparos and Lionel Marchetti, *Livre Des Morts*
Composed by Lionel Marchetti and Olivier Capparos; lyrics by C. T. Dreyer,
　Damia, Giacinto Scelsi, Luigi Nono, Paul Celan, Pierre Henry, Whitehouse
Entr'acte CD 2011, E53

Aleš Kacjan, *Flavta*
Music by various artists (Giacinto Scelsi, *Hyxos*)
ZKP RTVS CD 2011, 111853

Juho Laitinen, *Cello, Voice And Sampler*
Music by various artists (Giacinto Scelsi, *Maknongan*)
Tulkinnanvaraista CD 2011, TULK001

Marianne Pousseur, *Only*
Music by John Cage, Morton Feldman, Hanns Eisler, Giacinto Scelsi (*Hô 1,
　Hô 4*), György Kurtág, Henri Pousseur, Frederic Rzewski, Théodore Botrel,
　Rudolf Sieczynski
Sub Rosa CD 2011, SR278

Geneviève Strosser, *György Ligeti. Sonate Pour Alto*
Music by György Ligeti, Heinz Holliger, Franco Donatoni,
　Helmut Lachenmann, Giacinto Scelsi (*Manto I, II, III*)
Aeon CD 2011, AECD1100

Thomas Zehetmair, Ruth Killius, *Manto and Madrigals*
Music by Rainer Killius, Giacinto Scelsi (*Manto I, II, III*), Heinz Holliger,
　Bela Bartók, Nikos Skalkottas, Maxwell Davies, Bohuslav Martinů,
　Johannes Nied
EMC Records CD 2011, ECM New Series 2150

Manuel Zurria, *Loops4ever*
Music by Giacinto Scelsi (CD 1: *Maknongan for Bass Flute, Pwyll for Flute,
　with Sounds Recorded in Giacinto Scelsi's house in Rome*), Pauline Oliveros,
　Alvin Lucier, Alvin Curran, John Duncan, Ter Veldhuis, Eve Beglarian,
　Clarence Barlow, William Basinski, Frederic Rzewski, Terry Riley
Mazagran 2 CD 2011, MZ001

Sonia Wieder-Atherton, *Vita. Monteverdi and Scelsi*
Music by Claudio Monteverdi, Giacinto Scelsi (*Trilogy: Triphon, Dithome, Ygghur*)
Naïve CD 2011, V 5257

2012
Marches. Demilitarised Zones / Entmilitarisierte Zonen
Music by various artists (Giacinto Scelsi, *I Riti*)
Capriccio 2CD, C5121

Wittener Tage Für Neue Kammermusik 2012
Music by various artists (Giacinto Scelsi, *Incantesimi*)
Kulturforum Witten, 2 CD, WD 2012

Kreng, *Secret Thirteen Mix 038*
Music by various artists (Giacinto Scelsi, *Ixor, Preludi* - Serie I: 4. Moderato)
Secret Thirteen Journal MP3 (320 kbps) 2011, STJ 038

Giancarlo Schiaffini, *Schiaffini*
Music by various artists (Giacinto Scelsi, *Maknongan*) and
    Giancarlo Schiaffini
Auditorium Edizioni, 2 CD, AUD 04412

Dan Styffe, *Secret Memories*
Music by various artists (Giacinto Scelsi, *Mantram*)
Oslo Philharmonic Orchestra, with Jukka-Pekka Saraste
Simax Classics, CD, PSC 1324

Mike Svoboda, *Da Lontano*
Music by John Cage, Giacinto Scelsi (*Mantram*), Luigi Nono,
    Karlheinz Stockhausen
WERGO SACD (Hybrid) 2012, WER 6744 2

2013
Anthony Burr, *Anthony Burr*
Music by Giacinto Scelsi (*Tre pezzi, Preghiera per un'ombra*), Erik Ulman,
    Thomas Meadowcroft, John Rodgers, Helmut Lachenmann
Skirl Records, CD, Skirl CD 016

Deepchord, *RA.390*
Music by various artists (Giacinto Scelsi, *Quattro pezzi per orchestra* [2nd movement])
Resident Advisor, MP3 (320 kbps), RA.390

Einóma, *Secret Thirteen Mix 096*
Music by various artists (Giacinto Scelsi, *Konx-Om-Pax, Natura Renovatur*)
Secret Thirteen Journal, MP3 (320 kbps), STJ 096

Roger Heaton, *The Inner Time*
Music by Pierre Boulez, Giacinto Scelsi (*Ixor*), Horatiu Radulescu
Clarinet Classics, CD, CC0067

Loscil, *Secret Thirteen Mix 052*
Music by various artists (Giacinto Scelsi, *Alleluja For Violoncello Solo*)
Secret Thirteen Journal, MP3 (320 kbps), STJ 052

Roly Porter, *Secret Thirteen Mix 075*
Music by various artists (Giacinto Scelsi, *Hymnos*)
Secret Thirteen Journal, MP3 (320 kbps), STJ 075

2014
Verdi, Scelsi, Nono, Pizzetti, Petrassi. Italia
Music by Giuseppe Verdi, Luigi Nono, Ildebrando Pizzetti, Giacinto Scelsi (*TKRDG*), Goffredo Petrassi
SWR Vokalensemble Stuttgart, with Marcus Creed
SWR Music, CD, 93.329

James Ginzburg, Yair Elazar Glotman, *Secret Thirteen Mix 134*
Music by various artists (Giacinto Scelsi, *Dharana, Pranam II*)
Secret Thirteen Journal, MP3 (320 kbps), STJ 134

Alain Goudard, Ancuza Aprodu, Six voix solistes, *Frasi nella luce nascente*
Music by various artists (Giacinto Scelsi, *Chemin du rêve, Comme un cri traverse un cerveau*)
EMA Vinci, CD, 40019

2015
Noël Akchoté, Once New Music
Music by Alvin Lucier, John Cage, Earle Brown, Giacinto Scelsi
 (*L'âme ouverte*), John Adams
Noël Akchoté Downloads, MP3 (320 kbps), ONM-2

DJ S.Y.D, *Invisibles Pensées*
Music by various artists (Giacinto Scelsi, *Nuits II. Le reveil profond*,
 Robert Black)
Bruits De Fond, File FLAC Mixed, Dig it! 10

Matthew Gee, François Killian, *Paradiso e Inferno*
Music by various artists (Giacinto Scelsi, *Three Pieces For Trombone Solo*)
MG Music, CD, GEE01

Vainio & Vigroux, *FACT Mix 522*
Music by various artists (Giacinto Scelsi, *Anahit. Poème lyrique dédié à Venus*)
FACT Magazine, MP3 (320 kbps), FACT 522

Sounds Of Wergo
Music by various artists (Giacinto Scelsi, *Suite n. 10 "Ka,"* Sabine Liebner)
Neue Zeitschrift Für Musik - WERGO, CD, T 1566 2

Piano Works by Giacinto Scelsi (*Sonata per pianoforte 1942–1944*) and
 Vieri Tosatti
Donna Amato, piano
Carnegie Mellon University–School of Music CD 0115

2016
Scelsi EP
Music by various artists (Giacinto Scelsi, *Duo for violin and cello*)
SN Variations, LP, Mispress sn2

Giusy Caruso, *Scelsi, Putignano, Anzaghi. Piano Works*
Music by various artists (Giacinto Scelsi, *Suite n. 9 "Ttai"*)
Tactus, CD, TC.930001

Michele Marelli, *Contemporary Clarinet*
Music by various artists (Giacinto Scelsi, *Kya*)
Decca, CD, 4812772

Andreas Skouras, *Ins Offene. Klaviermusik Der Moderne / Piano Music Of Modern Age*
Musi bu Claude Debussy, Olivier Messiaen, Karlheinz Stockhausen, Pascal Dusapin, Giacinto Scelsi (*Four Illustrations On The Metamorphosis Of Vishnu*) et al.
NEOS, CD, NEOS 11610

2017
50 Jahre Steirischer Herbst + 50 Jahre Musikprotokoll = 100% Kultur Im ORF Steiermark
Music by various artists (Giacinto Scelsi [credit unknown])
ORF Studio Steiermark, DVD, ORFST-DVD-0121

Peter Katina, *Secrets*
Music by Arvo Pärt, Salvatore Sciarrino, Giacinto Scelsi (*In nomine lucis*), Edison Denisov, Iris Szeghy, John Cage
Hevhetia, CD, HV 0145-2-331

Rocco Parisi, Isabella Fabbri, *Scelsi Bach*
Music by Johann Sebastian Bach, Giacinto Scelsi (*Ixor, Maknongan, Tre pezzi*), Isabella Fabbri, Rocco Parisi
Digressione Music, CD, DIGR 76

Clément Saunier, *Directions*
Music by Peter Maxwell Davies, Giacinto Scelsi (*Quattro pezzi*), Hans Werner Henze, Toru Takemitsu, Ivan Fedele, Matthias Pintscher
Klarthe Records, CD, KLA058

Secret Pyramid, *Isolatedmix 74*
Music by various artists (Giacinto Scelsi, *String Quartet n. 3 - Avec une grande tendresse*)
A Strangely Isolated Place, MP3 (320 kbps), Isolatedmix 74

2018
Tom Curry, *Alight*
Music by various artists (Giacinto Scelsi, *Maknongan*)
With Vincent Fuh, and Iva Ugrčić
Summit Records, CD, DCD 718

Reinhold Friedrich, The Trumpet Collection
Music by various artists (Giacinto Scelsi, CD 7: *4 Stücke*)
Capriccio, 10 CD, C7285

Joëlle Léandre, *Double Bass*
Music by various artistis (Giacinto Scelsi, CD 1: *C'est bien la nuit,
    Le réveil profond, Maknongan*)
L'Empreinte Digitale, 2 CD, ED13250 (recto: reissue *Contrebasse et voix*,
    Adda, 581043, 1990, verso: reissue *Urban Bass*, Adda, 581254, 1991)

Michele Marelli, *Clarinet Reloaded*
Music by Ivan Fedele, Giacinto Scelsi (*Ixor*), Karlheinz Stockhausen,
    Michel Van Der Aa, Helmut Lachenmann
Decca, CD, 481 7271

2019
Pedro Pablo Cámara Toldos, *Solitaire. Solo Saxophone Masterpieces*
Music by various artists (Giacinto Scelsi, CD 1: *Tre pezzi*)
IBS Classical, 2 CD, IBS222018

Josè Daniel Cirigliano, *Musica per clarinetto solo dal XX al XXI secolo*
Music by Guido López Gavilán, Alessandra Ravera, Antonio Fraioli,
    William O. Smith, Bruno Bettinelli, Giacinto Scelsi (*Ixor II*),
    Giovanni Mattaliano
Tactus, CD, TC 930002

Lussuria, NE288
Music by various artists (Giacinto Scelsi, *Uaxuctum IV*)
Needle Exchange, MP3 (320 kbps), NE288

Santi Mabad, *Full Metal*
Music by Sergio Blardony, Franco Donatoni, Sergio Fidemraizer, Giacinto
Scelsi (*Maknongan*), Gerard Brophy, Ortiz Morales
Columna Musica, CD, 1CM0389

Alberto Napolitano, *Mutazioni. Sciarrino, Telemann, Napolitano, Scelsi,
    Debussy*
Music by various artists (Giacinto Scelsi, *Tre pezzi*)
Stradivarius, CD, STR 37126

Sara Stowe, *Ogloudoglou*
Music by Giacinto Scelsi (*Talagaru n. 4, Canto del Capricorno n. 8, Ogloudoglou, CKCKC*), John Cage, Sylvano Bussotti, Luciano Berio, Mauricio Kagel, Luigi Nono, Niccolò Castiglioni, Morton Feldman
Metier, CD, msv 28593

Gervasio Tarragona Valli, *Time After Yesterday. 20th And 21st Centuries Clarinet Masterworks Vol. 1*
Music by various artists (Giacinto Scelsi, *Ixor*)
Da Vinci Classics, CD, C00197

Voktett Hannover, *Liebesweisen*
Music by various artistis (Giacinto Scelsi, *Tre canti sacri: Gloria*)
Rondeau Production, CD, ROP6172

2020
SWR Vokalensemble, *Chormusik Der Welt / Choir Music Of The World*
Music by various artistis (Giacinto Scelsi, CD 3: *Yliam, TKRDG*)
With Marcus Creed
SWR Classic, 10 CD, SWR19100CD

2021
Alter Ego + Matmos, *Pranam. A(Round) Giacinto Scelsi*
Excerpts from *Quartetto per archi n. 3, Ko-Lho, Riti: I funerali di Carlo Magno, Aitsi*
Die Schachtel, LP / Flac, DS42/1

Dario Calderone, *Il Nuovo Contrabbasso Italiano*
Music by Luciano Berio, Giacinto Scelsi (*Le réveil profond*), Franco Donatoni, Salvatore Sciarrino, Stefano Scodanibbio
Stradivarius, CD, STR 37182

Yoko Morimyo, Damiano Afrifa, *Musica spirituale*
Music by Franco Battiato, Arvo Pärt, Giacinto Scelsi (*L'âme ailée*), Florence B. Price
19'40", CD, 19m40s_16

Index

the Absolute, 49
absolute subjectivism, 53
Adorno, Theodor W., 104
affectivity. *See* emotion and emotionality
African American music, 12, 38–39
African art, 12
African drumming, 36–37, 41
African music, 27
African rhythms, 34, 36–38
Aiôn, 69
d'Alessandro, Raffaele, 63
American Indian music, 38
Amphion (mythological), 23n2
Anahad, 81
André, Franz, 65
Anschluss (12 March 1938), 3
Appia, Adolphe, 8
Appia, Edmond, 5, 8–10
Arab music, 37
art: African, 12; creative artistic faculty and, 72, 90–92, 97; essence of, 89–90; knowledge and, 89, 100; movements, 93–96; Western, evolution of, 27
"Art and Knowledge" (Scelsi, G.), xi–xii, 71–73, 89–101

"Art and Satanism" (Scelsi, G.), 43–49
art critics, 90, 92–93
artists: Asian, 91; cognition of, 100; consciousness of, 99; creative faculties of, 72, 90–92, 97; crystallization of instance of duration by, 90–92, 101; four elements of spirit and, 100; identification faculty of, 98–100; milieu of, 92; perceptive faculties of, 99; Satanism and, 45–48; sensibility, 11; universe and, 47
the arts: Satanism in, 43–44, 47, 49; synthesis of, 51; unity of, 51, 53–54, 56
asceticism, 101
Asian artists, 91
Asian music, 26–27, 34, 36–37, 83
audiences, composers and, 15–16
aural sensibility, 57–58
automatism, 11, 45, 53, 93
d'Ayala Valva, Giuseppe, 3

Bach, J. S., 22, 35, 37–38, 42n6, 82–84
Baudelaire, Charles, 43, 45, 48, 49n3, 51, 93

Beausire, Pierre, 54–55
Beethoven, Ludwig van, 35, 83, 104
Berg, Alban, 5, 30, 62
Bergson, Henri, 46
bitonality, 26
blues, 39
Boehme, Jakob, 86
Borodin, Alexander, 34
Boulanger, Nadia, 63
Brémond, Henri, 43
Breton, André, 93–94
Buddhist music, 103
Burckhardt, C. J., 22
Burger, Paul, 5

Caffarelli, Filippo, 6
Cangemi, Giorgio, 65
Casa Eranos, annual colloquia at, 71
Cercles (Scelsi, G.), xvii, 104, 108
Le chant du rossignol, 37–38
Chopin, Frédéric, 29–30
chords, 17, 26, 28–30, 31n4
chromaticism, 5, 26, 30, 34
class consciousness, xii
Classicism, 28
Claudel, Paul, 23
clavioline, 72
cognition, 10, 54, 98, 100
collective consciousness, 36
color: sound and, 51–52, 86; as vibration, 80
Columbia University's Miller Theater, ix
composers: audiences and, 15–16; images projected through sound matter of, 15–16; on instruments and sounds, 83
consciousness: of artists, 48, 99; class, xii; collective, 36; in creation, 21, 23; four elements of spirit and, 97; images and, 16, 47, 54; mystical states of, 87, 99; perceptions and, 99; as physical and nonphysical, 98; rhythm and, 36–38; transfiguration and, 45; unity of the arts and, 53–54, 58; vibrations of matter and, 57
Coppola, Piero, 4–5, 13n2, 62
Cortot, Alfred, 63
cosmic unity, 58
Coué, Émile, 85
Council of Constantinople, 22
creative artistic faculty, 72, 90–92, 97
Cremonese, Adriano, xv–xvi, 13, 25, 31n5, 33

Dadaism, 94
Dallapiccola, Luigi, 63
Daniel-Rops, Henri, 49, 50n7
Debussy, Claude, 25–30, 31n4, 38–39; harmony of, 28–30, 34; rhythm of, 34, 38
de-composing and re-composing, 71
demonism, 43–46
De Santis, Edizioni, x, 61
Désormiere, Roger, 65
Devas, 85–86
Devic activity, x, 85–87
Devic dimension, 70
disorder, 46
dissonances, 29
Drillon, Jacques, 66
Drott, Eric, xv
drugs, 52
drumming: African, 36–37, 41; jazz, 39
Dukas, Paul, 27
duration, xii, 12, 72; artist crystallizing an instance of, 90–92, 101; motion and, 90–92; pitch and, 75, 80; rhythm and, 16–19, 36–37

Eigeldingen, Marc, 50n7
Elektra, 29
Ellington, Duke, 39
emotion and emotionality, 10–12, 16, 21–22; aural sensibility and, 57; as Emotional Element, of spirit, 97;

harmony and, 18; images and, 18–19, 29; intellect and, 18, 35, 70; melody and, 17–18; memory and, 57; rhythm and, 18
energy: sound as, 81–82; unity of, 52
engrams, 98
Eranos-Jahrbuch, 71
L'Evolution créatrice (Bergson), 46
"The Evolution of Harmony" (Scelsi, G.), x, 25–30, 69
"The Evolution of Rhythm" (Scelsi, G.), x–xi, xvi, 25, 33–41, 69
expressive atonality, 5

Falk, Richard, x, 5–7
Fauré, Gabriel, 23
Faust Symphony, 34
Les Fenêtres (Mallarmé), 48
The Firebird, 35
"forbidden" music, 48
form/structure, 16, 19, 31n4, 34, 82, 84
Futurism, 39–40

Gauguin, Paul, 55–56
geometric shapes, *108*, 108–9
German Jews, in Switzerland, 13n1
Gestapo, 4
God: Satanism and, 43–44, 47–49; universe and, 44
Goethe, 23, 80, 83
Gourmont, Remy de, 31, 46
Gouverné, Yvonne, 65
Guarneri, 83

harmonics, of sound, 75, 80, 83
harmony: Asian, 27; of Debussy, 28–30, 34; disorder and, 46; emotion and, 18; evolution of, 26, 29, 38, 70; images of, 17; melody and, 11–12, 16–19, 22, 39; psyche and, 30, 38; rhythm and, 17, 19, 27, 36–38, 40; Satanism and, 43; science of, 17; of Stravinsky, 35, 37–38; transfiguration and, 47; uselessness and, 46–47; of Wagner, 26, 28
Hasler, Alfred A., 13n1
Hindu music, 37, 103
L'Histoire du Soldat, 39, 41
Hitler, Adolf, 13n1

identification faculty, of artists, 98–100
identity of matter and spirit, 12
images: consciousness and, 16, 47, 54; emotion and, 18–19, 29; harmony and, 17; music and, 16; psychic and, 17, 19, 26, 29, 52; sound matter and, 15–16; structure and, 19; in subconscious, 53; virtual, 99
impressionism, 27
incantations, 85–86
Infernal Dance of Kastchei, 35
influences, 28
inner sounds, 80
instant of duration, xii, 90–92, 101
intelligence/intellect, 10–12, 16–22, 57–58; emotion and, 18, 35, 70; as Intellectual Element, of spirit, 97; melody and, 84

Jaecker, Friedrich, 13
japa, 85
jazz, xi, 35, 38–39, 41
just one word (*una parola sola*), 105

Kanach, Sharon, 13, 31n4
Kanach-Actes Sud, xvi
Klein, Walther, 5
knowledge: art and, 89, 100; total, 89

La Bruyère, Jean de, 21, 23n2
Lassueur, Charles, 5
Lattanzi, Mario, 65
Lausanne, Thursday 11 June 1942–XX concert and concert program, 3–6, 4, 8–9
Laya and Kriya-Yoga, 81

Liszt, Franz, 34, 64

machines, rhythm and, 39–40
Magaloff, Nikita, 5, 62–64
magic, 30
Mallarmé, Stéphane, 48, 54–55
Marinetti, Filippo Tommaso, 39
Maritain, Jacques, 43
Martin, Constant, 72
Martinis, Luciano, xvi, 25, 33, 104
The Mastersingers of Nuremberg, 34
matter, 12, 15–16, 57
Mazy, René, 65
"The Meaning of Music" (Scelsi, G.), 15–23
melody: emotion and, 17–18; harmony and, 11–12, 16–19, 22, 39; intellect and, 84; jazz, 38–39; Mozart and Wagner on, 22; rhythm and, 17–19; sound and, 18; spirit and, 22
memory, 57
Metzger, Heinz-Klaus, xv–xvi, 13
microtonal style, 103
moldable intonation, 71
moralities, 47–48
motion: duration and, 90–92; in painting, 94; rhythm and, 40–41; sound in, 69
Mozart, Wolfgang Amadeus, 22, 31n4, 35, 83–84
Music as Dream (Pellegrini and Sciannameo), xv
musico-historical progress, x–xi
Musik-Konzepte 31—Giacinto Scelsi (Metzger and Riehn), xv–xvi
Mussorgsky, Modest, 27–28
mystical states, of consciousness, 87, 99

La nascita del Verbo, 64–65, 103
nature, 44–46
Nazis, 13n1
neo-spiritualism, 12
Les Noces, 37–38, 41, 42n6

non-Euclidian geometry, 12
una nota sola (the single sound), xvii, 103, 105
note, sound and, 71, 81

objective understanding of music, 10, 16, 20–21
objectivism, 51
occultism, 30, 81
Octologo (Scelsi, G.), xvii, 104–5, 106–7
Oedipus Rex, 38
ondiola, 72, 103
Opera Omnia, 6

painting, 55–56, 80, 94–95
una parola sola (just one word), 105
Le parole gelate (Scelsi, G.), 105, 108
Parsifal, 27
Pellegrini, Carlotta Alessandra, xv–xvi
pentatonic scales, 27
perceptions, identification faculty for, 99
perceptual *apparati*, 56–57
Pergolesi, Giovan Battista, 6
Perrin, Maurice, 5
Petrushka, 35
phenomenology, 91
phenomenon of creation, 48
Piano Sonata op. 1, 62
Piano Trio, 6; *Andante*, 7, 7–9, 8, 9
pitch, duration and, 75, 80
Plato, 48–49, 104
poetic realism, 27
poetry, 95–96, 100, 104–5, 108
polemics, 93
post-Wagnerian music, x
Prometheus, 30, 51
Prometheus (mythological), 30, 35, 51, 64, 70, 72
psyche, 16; aural sensibility and, 58; emotion and intellect and, 18; harmony, 30, 38; memory and, 57; as Psychic Element, of spirit, 97; rhythm

and, 10–12, 19, 26–28; in unity of the arts, 53
psychic images, 17, 19, 26, 29, 52
psychism, 18–19, 21–22, 58

Quartetto per due violini, viola e violoncello, 64
Quattro pezzi per orchestra (ciascuno su una sola nota), 103
Quattro poemi, 62

Ramsden, Dorothy Kate, 3, 13n2, 61–62
Randolph's Folly, 13n2
rationalism, 22
Ravel, Maurice, 22
Reish, Gregory N., xvi
relativity, 12
rhythm: African, 34, 36–38; as alternation of sound and silence, 16, 35–36; Arab, 37; in Asian music, 37; consciousness and, 36–38; of Debussy, 34, 38; duration and, 16–19, 36–37; emotion and, 18; evolution of, 34–35, 38; harmony and, 17, 19, 27, 36–38, 40; of jazz, 35; machines and, 39–40; melody and, 17–19; memory and, 57; motion and, 40–41; psyche and, 10–12, 19, 26–28; in Russian music, 34; of Stravinsky, 34–38, 41nn3–4; syncopation, 34–35, 37, 41n4; time and, 16–17, 36–37; of universe, 36; as Vital Element, of spirit, 97; of Wagner, 34
rhythmic language, 16, 36–37, 40–41, 42n6
Ribot, Marc, ix
Riehn, Rainer, xv–xvi
Rimbaud, Arthur, 43, 48, 49n3, 51
The Rite of Spring, 34–38, 41, 41n4, 70
Rothmund, Heinrich, 4, 13n1
Rufer, Magdi, 63
running the sound, 71
Russian music, 26–28, 34–35

Said, Edward, 104
Sallustio, Giacinto, 5–6
Satanism: artists and, 45–48; in the arts, 43–44, 47, 49; God and, 43–44, 47–49; harmony and, 43; transfiguration and, 44–45
Scarpini, Pietro, 5
Scelsi, Fondazione Isabella, xvi–xvii
Scelsi, Giacinto: avant-garde concert music and, ix; birthday, 104; Circle and Line autographed signature, *108*; class consciousness of, xii; Coppola and, 4–5; as cryptic and enigmatic, ix–x; death of, 104; Falk and, 5–7; in Lausanne, x, 3–5, 33, 61–66, 70–71; Lausanne concert, 1942, 4–6; on musico-historical progress, x–xi; return to Rome, x, 61, 72; three periods of creative styles, 103–4. *See also specific topics; specific works*
Scelsi d'Ayala Valva, Giovanna, 6, 61, 64–65
Scelsi Morning, ix
Schaeffner, André, 41nn3–4
Schoenbergian system, 63
Schubert, Franz, 22
Schumann, Robert, 22, 31n4
Sciannameo, Franco, xv
science of harmony, 17
Scriabin, Alexander, 5, 30, 51, 62, 64
self, 45, 48
Sens de la musique (Scelsi, G.), xv–xvi, 9–13, 25
sensory organs, 58
shamanism, 81
silence and sound, alternation of, 16, 35–36
the single sound (*una nota sola*), xvii, 103, 105
Il sogno 101 (Scelsi, G.), xvi, 70–71, 108
Sonata for piano, 63–64
Sonata in B Minor, 64

soul, spirit and, 21–22, 97
sound: color and, 51–52, 86; as cosmic force, 81; as energy, 81–82; harmonics of, 75, 80, 83; images and, 15–16; inner, 80; instruments and, 83; melody and, 18; in motion, 69; music and, 72, 75, 82–83, 85–86; note and, 71, 81; of ondiola, 72; physiological perception of, 57; pitch and duration of, 75, 80; running the, 71; silence and, alternation of, 16, 35–36; spectrum of, 75; as spherical, 75, 80, 103–4; spirit and, 22; three dimensions of, 69, 75, 80, 103; vibration and, 71–72, 75, 81–82; Yoga of, 81
"Sound and Music" (Scelsi, G.), xi, 71–72, 76–79
sound therapy, 82
sound waves, 53–54, 75
space and time, 12, 37
spherical sound, 75, 80, 103–4
spirit: four fundamental elements of, 97, 100; identity of matter and, 12; melody and, 22; soul and, 21–22, 97; sound and, 22
spirituals, 39
Steiner, Rudolf, 20–21, 70
Stradivarius, 83
Strauss, Richard, 29
Stravinsky, Igor, 26, 39, 41, 42n6, 63, 70; harmony of, 35, 37–38; rhythms of, 34–38, 41nn3–4
Strawinsky (Schaeffner), 41nn3–4
String Quartet, 34
subconscious, 17, 45, 53, 57
subjectivism, 53
Suisse Contemporaine, xv, 13, 20–21, 25
Surrealism, 43, 45, 93–94
Swedenborg, Emanuel, 86
Switzerland: asylum in, 3–4; German Jews in, 13n1; Scelsi, G., in, x, 3–5, 33, 61–66, 70–71

symbolism, 27
Symphony of Psalms, 38
syncopation, 34–35, 37, 41n4
synthesis, of the arts, 51

Tanner, André, 20–21
tantric magic, 81
Tetratkys, 69
theme, in music, 95
theosophy, 12, 30
three dimensional sound, 69, 75, 80, 103
time, 12–13; jazz and, 39; rhythm and, 16–17, 36–37; space and, 12, 37
Tosatti, Vieri, 65, 103
total knowledge, 89
transfiguration, 43–45, 47, 108
The Transformation of Giacinto Scelsi's Musical Style and Aesthetic (Reish), xvi
Tribune de Lausanne, 8
Trio No. 2 per Violino, Violoncello e Pianoforte, 5, 9, 64
Tristan und Isolde, 27, 34
12 Preludi (prima serie), 62–63
twelve-tone system, 63

the unconscious, 21–22, 45, 93–94
unity: of the arts, 51, 53–54, 56; cosmic, 58; of energy or vibration, 52; psychophysical, 98
"Unity and Equality of the Arts" (Scelsi, G.), 51–58
universe: artists and, 47; celestial "hum" of, 104; evolution of, 87; God and, 44; phenomenology of, 91; rhythm of, 36
uselessness, 46–47

Van Bouwel, Jan, 65
vaporization, 93
Variazioni e Fuga, 63
Vedas, 81

vibrations, 16, 36, 51–53; artistic, 101; colors as, 80; the Divine and, 87; of matter, consciousness and, 57; sound and, 71–72, 75, 81–82
virtual images, 99
Voltaire, 22

Wagner, Richard, 27, 30, 55, 59n3; harmony of, 26, 28; melody of, 22; rhythms of, 34
Wagnerism, 26, 28–30, 34

Webern, Anton von, 63
whole-tone scale, 27, 29
Will, individual and universal, 55, 59n3
Winans, T. G., 62

Xnoybis, 69

Yoga, 81, 86, 89

Zafred, Mario, 65

About the Editors

FRANCO SCIANNAMEO is College of Fine Arts Distinguished Scholar & Teaching Professor of Music at Carnegie Mellon University in Pittsburgh, Pennsylvania (United States). He writes and lectures extensively on contemporary music and its relation to politics, cinema, and the arts. He has worked with several celebrated composers, including Giacinto Scelsi, Vieri Tosatti, Nino Rota, Franco Donatoni, Ennio Morricone, Franco Evangelisti, and Paul Chihara with whom he collaborated on performances and recordings. His books include *Nino Rota's The Godfather Trilogy* (Lanham: Rowman & Littlefield, 2010), *Phil Trajetta (1777–1854), Patriot, Musician, Immigrant, Music as Dream: Essays on Giacinto Scelsi*, edited with Alessandra Carlotta Pellegrini (Lanham: Rowman & Littlefield, 2013), *Experiencing the Violin Concerto: A Listener's Companion* (Lanham: Rowman & Littlefield, 2016); *Musicians' Migratory Patterns: The Adriatic Coasts, Reflections on the Music of Ennio Morricone: Fame and Legacy* (Lanham: Lexington Books, 2020), and *Italian Film Music, 1950s–1970s: Between Tradition, Innovation, and Internationalisation*, edited by Franco Sciannameo (forthcoming).

ALESSANDRA CARLOTTA PELLEGRINI is scientific director of Fondazione Isabella Scelsi (Rome), the universal heir to the artistic and cultural legacy of Italian composer Giacinto Scelsi (1905–1988), and professor of music history at the Conservatorio "Domenico Cimarosa" in Avellino, Italy.

Her main research interests are in Italian music of the twentieth century, and the archival musical sources of the nineteenth and twentieth centuries including the protection, conservation, enhancement, and management of the musical archival heritage.

Alessandra Carlotta Pellegrini has edited the autobiography of Giacinto Scelsi *Il sogno 101* in Italian and in French, and the volume *Music as Dream: Essays on Giacinto Scelsi* (Lanham: Rowman & Littlefield, 2013), with Franco Sciannameo. Furthermore, she has authored essays and edited volumes on Alfredo Casella, Giacinto Scelsi, Luigi Nono, Goffredo Petrassi, and Paul Hindemith for such scientific journals as *Archival Notes*, *MusikTexte*, *Filigrane*, *Musica / Realtà*, *New Italian Music Magazine* and for publishers like Quodlibet, Actes Sud, Rowman & Littlefield, LIM, Brepols, LIT Verlag, MusikTexte, Kappa, and Aracne.

www.ingramcontent.com/pod-product-compliance
Lightning Source LLC
Chambersburg PA
CBHW061450300426
44114CB00014B/1916